baby crochet

# baby crochet

## 20 hand crochet designs for babies 0-24 months

## Lois Daykin

### PHOTOGRAPHS BY JOHN HESELTINE

St. Martin's Griffin
New York

BABY CROCHET

www.stmartins.com

*Project editor* Susan Berry
*US editor* Sally Harding
*Designer* Anne Wilson
*Stylist* Susan Berry
*Patterns writing & checking* Sue Whiting, Tricia McKenzie

Library of Congress Cataloging-in-Publication Data Available Upon Request

ISBN-10: 0-312-36883-6
ISBN-13: 978-0-312-36883-8

Created by Berry & Co. (Publishing Ltd.) for Rowan Yarns
First U.S. Edition: August 2007

10 9 8 7 6 5 4 3 2 1

Reproduced and printed in Singapore.

# contents

# introduction

• • • • • • • • •

Everyone wants to make something personal for a new baby. A handmade gift is just about the nicest thing you can give to a much loved friend or relative to mark such a special occasion, so I have included a couple of gift wrapping ideas, too.

Crochet is now much more popular than it has been for ages. You can use crochet to make some really fantastic projects for young babies, in particular toys, nursery decorations, and accessories such as scarves, hats, and bootees. And you can use all the range of Rowan yarns, including wool and cotton, for your projects.

Once you have mastered the basic stitches in crochet, you can quickly start to make many of the items in this book, most of which have been designed in simple single or double crochet. There are a wide range of projects to choose from, including some that require only very basic skills, such as the little scarf and hat set, the simple wrap cardigan, and the hearts bunting.

I always think that crochet lends itself to quite bright colors because it has a more robust character than knitting; as a result, many of my designs feature brightly colored stripes or squares.

The great joy of crochet is that it grows quickly, and is also very portable. The texture of crochet is dense and hardwearing, so it is ideally suited to the kind of wear and tear it will get from little children.

I hope you have as much fun making the projects in this book as I did designing them.

# beanies

• • • • • • • • •

There is a girl's version and a boy's version of these little hats—one in pink and one in blue. The simple beanie design with a striped border is worked in supersoft Rowan *RYC Cashsoft*. For decoration on the crown, you can opt for a three-dimensional flower motif made with the four colors in the hat (shown on the girl's version on page 12), or for a jaunty chain-stitch tassel (shown on the boy's version on page 13).

Worked in the round from the brim to the crown, the hats are very easy to crochet and make a good project for a relative beginner.

**To fit age, approximately**

| 0–3 | 3–6 | 6–12 | months |
|------|------|------|--------|

**Finished measurements**

**WIDTH AROUND HEAD**

| 13 | 14½ | 15½ | in |
|------|------|------|--------|
| 33 | 37 | 40 | cm |

## Yarns

### GIRL'S VERSION

1 (1: 1) x 50g/1¾oz ball of Rowan *RYC Cashsoft Baby DK* in
**MC** (Pixie 807)

1 (1: 1) x 50g/1¾oz ball of *Rowan RYC Cashsoft DK* in each
of **A** (Crush 506), **B** (Poison 513), and **C** (Bloom 520)

1 (1: 1) x 50g/1¾oz ball of Rowan *RYC Cashsoft 4 ply* in
**D** (Rose Lake 421)

### BOY'S VERSION

1 (1: 1) x 50g/1¾oz ball of Rowan *RYC Cashsoft DK* in each
of **MC** (Cream 500) and **B** (Donkey 517)

1 (1: 1) x 50g/1¾oz ball of Rowan *RYC Cashsoft Baby DK* in
each of **A** (Blue Boy 809), **C** (Cloud 805), and **D** (Chicory 804)

## Hook

Size G-6 (4mm) crochet hook

## Gauge

18 sts and 12½ rows to 4in/10cm measured over patt using
size G-6 (4mm) hook *or size to obtain correct gauge*.

## Abbreviations

**dc2tog** = [yo and insert hook in next st, yo and draw
loop through, yo and draw through 2 loops] twice, yo
and draw through all 3 loops on hook; **dc3tog** = [yo and
insert hook in next st, yo and draw loop through, yo
and draw through 2 loops] 3 times, yo and draw
through all 4 loops on hook.
See also page 117.

## To make

Using size G-6 (4mm) hook and A, ch 60 (66: 72) and join
with a slip st to first ch to form a ring.

**Round 1 (RS)** Using A, ch 1 (does NOT count as st), 1 sc in
each ch to end, 1 slip st in first sc. 60 (66: 72) sts.

**Round 2** Using A, ch 1 (does NOT count as st), 1 sc in each sc
to end, 1 slip st in first sc.

Break off A and join in B.

**Round 3** Using B, ch 1 (does NOT count as st), 1 sc in each sc
to end, 1 slip st in first sc.

Join in C.

**Round 4** Using C, ch 3 (counts as first dc), skip sc at base
of 3 ch, 1 dc in each sc to end, 1 slip st in top of 3 ch at beg
of round.

Break off C.

**Round 5** Using B, ch 1 (does NOT count as st), 1 sc in each dc
to end, 1 slip st in first sc.

Join in D.

**Round 6** Using D, ch 3 (counts as first dc), skip sc at base of
3 ch, 1 dc in each sc to end, 1 slip st in top of 3 ch at beg of
round.

Break off D.

**Round 7** As round 5.

Break off B, join in MC and cont using MC only.

**Round 8** Ch 3 (counts as first dc), skip sc at base of 3 ch, 1 dc
in each sc to end, 1 slip st in top of 3 ch at beg of round.

**Round 9** Ch 1 (does NOT count as st), 1 sc in each dc to end,
1 slip st in first sc.

Rep last 2 rounds 1 (1: 2) times more.

### 1ST SIZE ONLY

**Round 11** As round 8.

### 3RD SIZE ONLY

**Next round** Ch 3 (counts as first dc), skip sc at base of 3 ch,
1 dc in each of next 9 sc, [dc2tog over next 2 sc, 1 dc in each
of next 10 sc] 5 times, dc2tog over last 2 sc, 1 slip st in top of
3 ch at beg of round. 66 sts.

**Next round** As round 9.

**2ND AND 3RD SIZES ONLY**

**Next round** Ch 3 (counts as first dc), skip sc at base of 3 ch, 1 dc in each of next 8 sc, [dc2tog over next 2 sc, 1 dc in each of next 9 sc] 5 times, dc2tog over last 2 sc, 1 slip st in top of 3 ch at beg of round. 60 sts.

**ALL SIZES**

**Next round** Ch 1 (does NOT count as st), 1 sc in each of first 8 dc, [sc2tog over next 2 sts, 1 sc in each of next 8 dc] 5 times, sc2tog over next 2 sts, 1 slip st in first sc. 54 sts.

**Next round** Ch 3 (counts as first dc), skip sc at base of 3 ch, 1 dc in each of next 5 sc, [dc3tog over next 3 sts, 1 dc in each of next 6 sc] 5 times, dc3tog over last 3 sts, 1 slip st in top of 3 ch at beg of round. 42 sts.

**Next round** Ch 1 (does NOT count as st), 1 sc in each of first 5 dc, [sc2tog over next 2 sts, 1 sc in each of next 5 dc] 5 times, sc2tog over next 2 sts, 1 slip st in first sc. 36 sts.

**Next round** Ch 3 (counts as first dc), skip sc at base of 3 ch, 1 dc in each of next 2 sc, [dc3tog over next 3 sts, 1 dc in each of next 3 sc] 5 times, dc3tog over last 3 sts, 1 slip st in top of 3 ch at beg of round. 24 sts.

**Next round** Ch 1 (does NOT count as st), 1 sc in each of first 2 dc, [sc2tog over next 2 sts, 1 sc in each of next 2 dc] 5 times, sc2tog over next 2 sts, 1 slip st in first sc. 18 sts.

**Next round** Ch 3 (does NOT count as st), skip sc at base of 3 ch, dc2tog over next 2 sc, [dc3tog over next 3 sts] 5 times, 1 slip st in dc2tog at beg of round. 6 sts.

**Next round** Ch 1 (does NOT count as st), [sc2tog over next 2 sts] 3 times, 1 slip st in first sc2tog. 3 sts.

Fasten off.

## Finishing
Press lightly on WS following instructions on yarn label.

## Flower motif for girl's hat
### FIRST PETAL LAYER
Using size G-6 (4mm) hook and B, ch 6 and join with a slip st to first ch to form a ring.

Join in A.

**Round 1** [Using B ch 22, 1 sc in ring, using A ch 22, 1 sc in ring] 6 times.

Fasten off.

### SECOND PETAL LAYER
Using size G-6 (4mm) hook and C, ch 6 and join with a slip st to first ch to form a ring.

Join in D.

**Round 1** [Using C ch 22, 1 sc in ring, using D ch 22, 1 sc in ring] 6 times.

Fasten off.

### THIRD PETAL LAYER
Using size G-6 (4mm) hook and B, ch 4 and join with a slip st to first ch to form a ring.

Join in A.

**Round 1** [Using B ch 22, 1 sc in ring, using A ch 22, 1 sc in ring] 3 times. Fasten off.

Lay Second Petal Layer on top of first petal layer, then third petal layer on top of these 2 layers and sew together at center. Attach completed flower to top of hat.

**Tassel for boy's hat**
**TASSEL STRANDS** (make 20)
Using size G-6 (4mm) hook and A, ch 30 and fasten off, trimming both cut yarn ends to about ½in/12mm. Make another 19 tassel strands in this way, making 4 more using A, and 5 using each of B, C, and D.
**TASSEL BASE**
Using size G-6 (4mm) hook and D, ch 1, [1 slip st in center of tassel strand in D, 1 slip st in center of tassel strand in C, 1 slip st in center of tassel strand in B, 1 slip st in center of tassel strand in A] 5 times.
Fasten off.
Roll up tassel base to form tassel and stitch in place, wrapping a length of D around base of tassel. Attach completed tassel to top of hat.

# building blocks

These soft crochet building blocks, each side with a different design, are fun to crochet and fun for little babies to play with, too. Each square is made from a fabric-covered block of foam rubber, which is covered with six crochet squares. The squares are quite large—each measures 6 inches (15cm).

The colorways I have chosen have a retro feel as they are bold and bright, but if you want a more typically "baby" palette for them, pick colors that tone closely together, for example the colors chosen for the string of hearts on pages 58 and 59.

Make as many as you wish!

## Size
Each building block is a 4¾in/12cm cube.

## Yarns
1 x 50g/1¾oz ball of Rowan *RYC Cashsoft DK* in each of
**A** (Clementine 510), **B** (Lime 509), **C** (Ballad Blue 508),
**D** (Bloom 520), **E** (Madame 511), **H** (Glacier 504), and
**J** (Poison)
1 x 50g/1¾oz ball of Rowan *RYC Cashsoft Baby DK* in each
of **F** (Imp 803) and **G** (Pixie 807)
**Note:** This yarn is sufficient for 4 complete blocks.

## Hook
Size G-6 (4mm) crochet hook

## Extras
One fabric-covered 4¾in/12cm foam cube for each block

## Gauge
Each motif measures 4¾in/12cm square using size G-6
(4mm) hook *or size to obtain correct gauge.*

## Abbreviations
**WP** = ch 6, 1 sc in 2nd ch from hook, 1 hdc in next ch,
1 dc in next ch, 1 tr in next ch, 1 dtr in next ch; **dtr2tog** =
*[yo] 3 times, insert hook as indicated, yo and draw loop
through, [yo and draw through 2 loops] 3 times, rep from *
once more, yo and draw through all 3 loops on hook; **sc3tog**
= [insert hook in next st, yo and draw loop through] 3 times,
yo and draw through all 4 loops on hook; **dc3tog** = [yo and
insert hook in next st, yo and draw loop through, yo and
draw through 2 loops] 3 times, yo and draw through all 4
loops on hook; **dc4tog** = [yo and insert hook in next st, yo
and draw loop through, yo and draw through 2 loops] 4
times, yo and draw through all 5 loops on hook; **dc7tog** =
[yo and insert hook in next st, yo and draw loop through, yo

and draw through 2 loops] 7 times, yo and draw through all
8 loops on hook.
See also page 117.

## Panel A
Using size G-6 (4mm) hook and A, ch 4 and join with a slip
st to first ch to make a ring.
**Round 1 (RS)** Using A, ch 3 (counts as 1 dc), 2 dc in ring, [ch
2, 3 dc in ring] 3 times, ch 2, 1 slip st in top of 3 ch at beg of
round.
Fasten off.
**Round 2** Join in B in one ch sp, ch 3 (counts as 1 dc), 2 dc in
same ch sp, *ch 1, skip 3 dc**, [3 dc, ch 2 and 3 dc] in next
ch sp, rep from * to end, ending last rep at **, 3 dc in same
ch sp as used for (ch 3 and 2 dc) at beg of round, ch 2, 1 slip
st in top of 3 ch at beg of round.
Fasten off.
**Round 3** Join in C in one corner ch sp, ch 3 (counts as 1 dc),
2 dc in same ch sp, *ch 1, skip 3 dc, 3 dc in next ch sp, ch 1,
skip 3 dc**, [3 dc, ch 2 and 3 dc] in next corner ch sp, rep
from * to end, ending last rep at **, 3 dc in same ch sp as
used for (ch 3 and 2 dc) at beg of round, ch 2, 1 slip st in top
of 3 ch at beg of round.
Fasten off.
**Round 4** Join in D in one corner ch sp, ch 3 (counts as 1 dc),
2 dc in same ch sp, *[ch 1, skip 3 dc, 3 dc in next ch sp]
twice, ch 1, skip 3 dc**, [3 dc, ch 2 and 3 dc] in next corner
ch sp, rep from * to end, ending last rep at **, 3 dc in same
ch sp as used for (ch 3 and 2 dc) at beg of round, ch 2, 1 slip
st in top of 3 ch at beg of round.
Fasten off.
**Round 5** Join in E in one corner ch sp, ch 3 (counts as 1 dc),
2 dc in same ch sp, *[ch 1, skip 3 dc, 3 dc in next ch sp] 3
times, ch 1, skip 3 dc**, [3 dc, ch 2 and 3 dc] in next corner
ch sp, rep from * to end, ending last rep at **, 3 dc in same
ch sp as used for (ch 3 and 2 dc) at beg of round, ch 2, 1 slip

st in top of 3 ch at beg of round.
Fasten off.

**Round 6** Join in J to one corner ch sp,
ch 1 (does NOT count as st), 3 sc in
corner ch sp, *[1 sc in each of next
3 dc, 1 sc in next ch sp] 4 times, 1 sc
in each of next 3 dc**, 6 sc in next
corner ch sp, rep from * to end,
ending last rep at **, 3 sc in same
corner ch sp as used for first 3 sc,
1 slip st in first sc.
Fasten off.

## Panel B

Using size G-6 (4mm) hook and F, ch 4
and join with a slip st to first ch to
make a ring.

**Round 1 (RS)** Ch 5 (counts as 1 dc and
2 ch), [3 dc in ring, ch 2] 3 times, 2 dc
in ring, 1 slip st in 3rd of 5 ch at beg
of round.

**Round 2** Slip st in first (corner) ch sp,
ch 7 (counts as 1 dc and 4 ch), 2 dc in
same ch sp, *1 dc in each of next
3 dc**, [2 dc, ch 4 and 2 dc] in next
(corner) ch sp, rep from * to end,
ending last rep at **, 1 dc in same ch
sp as used for slip st at beg of round,
1 slip st in 3rd of 7 ch at beg of round.

**Round 3** Slip st in first (corner) ch sp,
ch 7 (counts as 1 dc and 4 ch), 2 dc in
same ch sp, *1 dc in each of next
7 dc**, [2 dc, ch 4 and 2 dc] in next
(corner) ch sp, rep from * to end,
ending last rep at **, 1 dc in same ch
sp as used for slip st at beg of round,

1 slip st in 3rd of 7 ch at beg of round.
Break off F and join in A.

**Round 4** Slip st in first (corner) ch sp, ch 7 (counts as 1 dc and 4 ch), 2 dc in same ch sp, *1 dc in each of next 11 dc**, [2 dc, ch 4 and 2 dc] in next (corner) ch sp, rep from * to end, ending last rep at **, 1 dc in same ch sp as used for slip st at beg of round, 1 slip st in 3rd of 7 ch at beg of round.

**Round 5** Slip st in first (corner) ch sp, ch 7 (counts as 1 dc and 4 ch), 2 dc in same ch sp, *1 dc in each of next 15 dc**, [2 dc, ch 4 and 2 dc] in next (corner) ch sp, rep from * to end, ending last rep at **, 1 dc in same ch sp as used for slip st at beg of round, 1 slip st in 3rd of 7 ch at beg of round.

Fasten off A and join in J to one corner ch sp.

**Round 6** Ch 1 (does NOT count as st), 3 sc in corner ch sp where yarn was rejoined, *1 sc in each of next 19 sc**, 6 sc in next corner ch sp, rep from * to end, ending last rep at **, 3 sc in same corner ch sp as used for first 3 sc, 1 slip st in first sc. Fasten off.

*gallery of projects*

**Panel C**

Using size G-6 (4mm) hook and A, ch 27.

**Row 1 (RS)** 1 sc in 2nd ch from hook, 1 sc in next ch, *skip 3 ch**, 7 dc in next ch, skip 3 ch, 1 sc in each of next 3 ch, rep from * to end, ending last rep at **, 4 dc in last ch, turn. 2½ patt reps.

Join in F.

**Row 2** Using F, ch 1 (does NOT count as st), 1 sc in each of first 2 dc, *ch 3**, dc7tog over next 7 sts, ch 3, 1 sc in each of next 3 dc, rep from * to end, ending last rep at **, dc4tog over last 4 sts, turn.

**Row 3** Using F, ch 3 (counts as first dc), 3 dc in st at base of 3 ch, *skip 3 ch**, 1 sc in each of next 3 sc, skip 3 ch, 7 dc in next dc7tog, rep from * to end, ending last rep at **, 1 sc in each of last 2 sc, turn.

**Row 4** Using A, ch 3 (does NOT count as st), skip sc at base of 3 ch, dc3tog over next 3 sts, *ch 3**, 1 sc in each of next 3 dc, ch 3, dc7tog over next 7 sts, rep from * to end, ending last rep at **, 1 sc in next dc, 1 sc in top of 3 ch at beg of previous row, turn.

**Row 5** Using A, ch 1 (does NOT count as st), 1 sc in each of first 2 sc, *skip 3 ch**, 7 dc in next dc7tog, skip 3 ch, 1 sc in each of next 3 sc, rep from * to end, ending last rep at **, 4 dc in dc3tog at beg of previous row, turn.

**Rows 6 to 9** As rows 2 to 5.

**Rows 10 to 12** As rows 2 to 4.

Break off A and join in J.

**Edging round (RS)** Ch 1 (does NOT count as st), 2 sc in st at base of 1 ch, 1 sc in next sc, 2 sc in next ch sp, [1 sc in next dc7tog, 3 sc in next ch sp, 1 sc in each of next 3 sc, 3 sc in next ch sp] twice, 3 sc in dc3tog at beg of previous row, work 23 sc evenly down row-end edge to foundation ch edge, 3 sc in first (corner) foundation ch, [3 sc in next ch sp, 1 sc in each of next 3 ch, 3 sc in next ch sp, 1 sc in next ch] twice, 2 sc in next ch sp, 1 sc in next ch, 3 sc in next (corner) ch, work 23 sc evenly up other row-end edge, 1 sc in same place as 2 sc at beg of round, 1 slip st in first sc. Fasten off.

## Panel D

Work as for Panel B, but using H in place of F and B in place of A.

## Panel E

Using size G-6 (4mm) hook and E, ch 26.

**Row 1 (RS)** 1 dc in 4th ch from hook, 1 dc in each ch to end, turn. 24 sts.

Join in D.

**Row 2** Using D, ch 3 (counts as 1 dc), skip dc at base of 3 ch, 1 dc in each dc to end, working last dc in top of 3 ch at beg of previous row, turn.

Join in G.

**Row 3** Using G, ch 3 (counts as 1 dc), skip dc at base of 3 ch, 1 dc in each dc to end, working last dc in top of 3 ch at beg of previous row, turn.

**Row 4** Using E, ch 3 (counts as 1 dc), skip dc at base of 3 ch, 1 dc in each dc to end, working last dc in top of 3 ch at beg

of previous row, turn.

**Rows 5 to 10** As rows 2 to 4, twice.

Break off E, D and G, and join in J.

**Edging round (RS)** Ch 1 (does NOT count as st), 2 sc in st at base of 1 ch, 1 sc in each of next 22 dc, 2 sc in top of 3 ch at beg of row 10, work 24 sc evenly down row-end edge to foundation ch edge, 2 sc in first (corner) foundation ch, 1 sc in each of next 22 foundation ch, 2 sc in next (corner) ch, work 24 sc evenly up other row-end edge, 1 slip st in first sc. Fasten off.

## Panel F

Using size G-6 (4mm) hook and C, ch 26.

**Row 1 (RS)** 1 sc in 2nd ch from hook, *1 WP, skip 5 ch, 1 sc in next ch, rep from * to end, turn. 25 sts, 4 patt reps.

Join in B.

**Row 2** Using B, ch 5 (counts as 1 dtr), *1 sc in top of WP, now work down side of WP working in ch as foll: 1 sc in next ch, 1 hdc in next ch, 1 dc in next ch, 1 tr in next ch**, 1 dtr in next ch, skip next sc, rep from * to end, ending last rep at **, dtr2tog over last ch of last WP and next sc, turn.

**Row 3** Using B, ch 1 (does NOT count as st), 1 sc in dtr2tog at end of previous row, *1 WP, skip 5 sts, 1 sc in next dtr, rep from * to end, working last sc in top of 5 ch at beg of previous row, turn.

Rows 2 and 3 form patt.

Join in H.

Using H, work 2 rows.

Break off H.

Using B, work 2 rows.

Break off B.

Using C, work 1 row.

Break off C and join in J.

**Edging round (RS)** Ch 1 (does NOT count as st), work 25 sc evenly along each side of Panel, 1 slip st in first sc. Fasten off.

## Heart

Using size G-6 (4mm) hook and B, ch 2.

**Row 1 (RS)** 3 sc in 2nd ch from hook, turn. 3 sts.

**Row 2** Ch 1 (does NOT count as st), 2 sc in first sc, 1 sc in next sc, 2 sc in last sc, turn. 5 sts.

**Row 3** Ch 1 (does NOT count as st), 2 sc in first sc, 1 sc in each of next 3 sc, 2 sc in last sc, turn. 7 sts.

**Row 4** Ch 1 (does NOT count as st), 1 sc in each sc to end, turn.

**Row 5** Ch 1 (does NOT count as st), 2 sc in first sc, 1 sc in each of next 5 sc, 2 sc in last sc, turn. 9 sts.

**Row 6** As row 4.

**Row 7** Ch 1 (does NOT count as st), 2 sc in first sc, 1 sc in each of next 7 sc, 2 sc in last sc, turn. 11 sts.

**Rows 8 to 10** As row 4.

**Row 11** Ch 1 (does NOT count as st), sc2tog over first 2 sc, 1 sc in each of next 3 sc and turn, leaving rem 6 sts unworked.

**Row 12** Ch 1 (does NOT count as st), [sc2tog over next 2 sts] twice. Fasten off.

Return to row 10, skip 1 sc at center, rejoin yarn to next sc and cont as foll:

**Row 11** Ch 1 (does NOT count as st), 1 sc in each of next 3 sc, sc2tog over last 2 sc, turn.

**Row 12** Ch 1 (does NOT count as st), [sc2tog over next 2 sts] twice.

Fasten off.

With RS facing, using size G-6 (4mm) hook and E, attach yarn to base of heart, ch 1 (does NOT count as st), 3 sc in base of heart, work in sc evenly around entire heart shape, working sc3tog at point where top sections meet and ending with 1 slip st in first sc. Fasten off.

Sew Heart onto center of Panel B.

## Star

Using size G-6 (4mm) hook and E, ch 5 and join with a slip st to first ch to form a ring.

**Round 1** Ch 1 (does NOT count as st), 15 sc in ring, 1 slip st in first sc. 15 sts.

**Round 2** Ch 1 (does NOT count as st), 1 sc in first sc, *ch 5, 1 sc in 2nd ch from hook, 1 hdc in next ch, 1 dc in next ch, 1 tr in next ch, skip 2 sc of round 1, 1 sc in next sc, rep from * to end, replacing sc at end of last rep with 1 slip st in first sc. Fasten off.

Sew Star onto center of Panel D.

## Finishing

Press lightly on WS following instructions on yarn label.

Using photograph as a guide and J, sew panels together around foam cube.

# flower motifs

• • • • • • • • •

This pretty little multilayered flower is very versatile and quick and easy to make. You can crochet a few and attach a clothespin to the back of each one, then use them to make a clothespin board for the nursery—pefect for hanging up baby's clothes or first drawings. With a pin at the back, they also make a good decoration to pin onto a gift bag.

The flower variation makes a great hair accessory (see page 27), and could be turned into a cute brooch for a cardigan, too.

To add interest, crochet the little black and gold bee to decorate your flowers (seen in close-up on page 25).

# multilayered flowers

## Size
Finished board is 3in/7.5cm wide and 18in/45cm long.

## Yarns
1 x 50g/1¾oz ball of Rowan *RYC Cashcotton 4 ply* in each of
**A** (Limone 907) and **B** (Imp 905)
1 x 50g/1¾oz ball of Rowan *4 ply Cotton* in each of
**C** (Cheeky 133) and **D** (Bloom 132)

## Hook
Size D-3 (3mm) crochet hook

## Extras
Wooden board 3in/7.5cm by 18in/45cm
3 wooden clothespins
Small amount of latex paint
Strong glue
Firm cardboard

## Gauge
Completed flower measures 3¼in/8.5cm in diameter using
size D-3 (3mm) hook *or size to obtain correct gauge.*

## Abbreviations
See page 117.

## Flower petals (make 3)
Using size D-3 (3mm) hook and A, ch 6 and join with a slip
st to first ch to form a ring.
**Round 1 (RS)** Ch 1 (does NOT count as st), 16 sc in ring,
1 slip st in first sc. 16 sts.
**Round 2** Ch 4 (counts as 1 hdc and 2 ch), skip sc at base of
4 ch and next sc, *1 hdc in next sc, ch 2, skip 1 sc, rep from
* to end, 1 slip st in 2nd of 4 ch at beg of round.

**Round 3** [1 slip st, 1 hdc, 1 dc, 1 hdc and 1 slip st] in each ch
sp to end, 1 slip st in first slip st. 8 petals.
Fasten off.
Working behind petals of previous round, attach B to base of
one dc at center of one petal and cont as foll:
**Round 4** Working behind petals of previous round: ch 1 (does
NOT count as st), 1 sc in place where yarn was rejoined, *ch 3,
1 sc in base of dc at center of next petal; rep from * to end,
replacing sc at end of last rep with 1 slip st in first sc.
**Round 5** [1 slip st, 1 hdc, 3 dc, 1 hdc and 1 slip st] in each ch
sp to end, 1 slip st in first slip st. 8 petals.
Fasten off.
Working behind petals of previous round, attach C to base of
center dc at center of one petal and cont as foll:
**Round 6** Working behind petals of previous round: ch 1 (does
NOT count as st), 1 sc in place where yarn was rejoined, *ch 4,
1 sc in base of dc at center of next petal; rep from * to end,
replacing sc at end of last rep with 1 slip st in first sc.
**Round 7** [1 slip st, 1 hdc, 5 dc, 1 hdc and 1 slip st] in each ch
sp to end, 1 slip st in first slip st. 8 petals.
Fasten off.
Working behind petals of previous round, attach D to base of
center dc at center of one petal and cont as foll:
**Round 8** Working behind petals of previous round: ch 1 (does
NOT count as st), 1 sc in place where yarn was rejoined, *ch 5,
1 sc in base of dc at center of next petal; rep from * to end,
replacing sc at end of last rep with 1 slip st in first sc.
**Round 9** [1 slip st, 1 hdc, 7 dc, 1 hdc and 1 slip st] in each ch
sp to end, 1 slip st in first slip st. 8 petals.
Fasten off.

## Flower centers (make 3)
Using size D-3 (3mm) hook and D, ch 2.
**Round 1 (RS)** 4 sc in 2nd ch from hook, 1 slip st in first sc.
4 sts.
**Round 2** Ch 1 (does NOT count as st), 2 sc in each sc to end,

1 slip st in first sc. 8 sts.

**Round 3** Ch 1 (does NOT count as st), 1 sc in each sc to end, 1 slip st in first sc.

**Round 4** Ch 1 (does NOT count as st), [sc2tog over next 2 sc] 4 times, 1 slip st in first sc2tog. Fasten off, leaving a long end.

### Finishing

Do NOT press.

Run a gathering thread around top of last round of flower centers, pull up tight and fasten off securely. Sew flower centers in place to center of flowers.

Lay Flowers on firm cardboard and cut out shape, then glue to cutouts. Using latex paint, paint wooden board and clothespins. Once dry, attach Flowers to clothespins, then clothespins to wooden board at intervals, facing downward.

If desired, make one Bee and attach to one Flower as in photograph.

## bee

### Size

Bee measures approximaely 1¼in/3cm long.

### Yarns

1 x 10g/³/₈oz ball of Coats *Pearl Cotton 8* in each of **A** (yellow 302), **B** (black 403), and **C** (white 1)

### Hook

Size 6 steel (1.5mm) crochet hook

### Extras

Scrap of washable toy filling

**Bee body** (make 1)

Using size 6 steel (1.5mm) hook and A, ch 2.

**Round 1 (RS)** 5 sc in 2nd ch from hook, 1 slip st in first sc, turn. 5 sts.

**Round 2** Ch 1 (does NOT count as st), 2 sc in each sc to end, 1 slip st in first sc, turn. 10 sts.

**Round 3** Ch 1 (does NOT count as st), 1 sc in each sc to end, 1 slip st in first sc, turn.

Join in B.

**Round 4** Using B, ch 1 (does NOT count as st), [1 sc in next sc, 2 sc in next sc] 5 times, 1 slip st in first sc, turn. 15 sts.

**Round 5** Using B, ch 1 (does NOT count as st), 1 sc in each sc to end, 1 slip st in first sc, turn.

**Rounds 6 and 7** Using A, ch 1 (does NOT count as st), 1 sc in each sc to end, 1 slip st in first sc, turn.

**Rounds 8 and 9** As round 5, twice.

**Rounds 10 and 11** As rounds 6 and 7.

**Round 12** As round 5.

**Round 13** Using B, ch 1 (does NOT count as st), [1 sc in next sc, sc2tog over next 2 sc] 5 times, 1 slip st in first sc, turn. 10 sts.

Break off B and cont using A only.

**Round 14** As round 3.

Insert a little toy filling inside bee.

**Round 15** Ch 1 (does NOT count as st), [sc2tog over next 2 sc] 5 times, 1 slip st in first sc, turn. 5 sts.

**Round 16** Ch 1 (does NOT count as st), 1 sc in first st, [sc2tog over next 2 sts] twice, 1 slip st in first sc. 3 sts.
Fasten off.

**Wings** (make 2)

Using size 6 steel (1.5mm) hook and C, ch 3.

**Row 1 (RS)** 2 sc in 2nd ch from hook, 2 sc in next ch, turn. 4 sts.

**Row 2** Ch 1 (does NOT count as st), 2 sc in first sc, 1 sc in each of next 2 sc, 2 sc in last sc, turn. 6 sts.

**Rows 3 and 4** Ch 1 (does NOT count as st), 1 sc in each sc to end, turn.

**Row 5** Ch 1 (does NOT count as st), sc2tog over first 2 sc, 1 sc in each of next 2 sc, sc2tog over last 2 sc, turn. 4 sts.

**Row 6** Ch 1 (does NOT count as st), sc2tog over first 2 sts, sc2tog over last 2 sts. 2 sts.
Fasten off, leaving a long end.

**Finishing**

Using photograph as a guide, embroider French knot eyes onto bees using C. Attach wings to bees, then attach bees to flower as in photograph.

## hair-decoration flower

**Size**

Finished flower is 1¼in/3cm in diameter.

**Yarns**

1 x 10g/³⁄₈oz ball of Coats *Pearl Cotton 8* in each of **A** (white 1) and **B** (pink 50)

**Hook**

Size 6 steel (1.5mm) crochet hook

**Extras**

8 tiny pink beads for each flower
Hairclips or elastic hairbands

**Gauge**

First 2 rounds measure ¾in/18mm in diameter using size 6 steel (1.5mm) hook *or size to obtain correct gauge*.

**Abbreviations**

**beaded ch** = slide bead up yarn so that it rests next to last st

worked, yarn over hook and draw loop through, securing bead on back of work.
See also page 117.

## To make

Thread 8 beads onto A.

Using size 6 steel (1.5mm) hook and A, ch 6 and join with a slip st to first ch to form a ring.

**Round 1 (WS)** Ch 1 (does NOT count as st), [1 sc in ring, 1 beaded ch] 8 times, 1 slip st in first sc, turn. 16 sts.

**Round 2 (RS)** Ch 4 (counts as 1 hdc and 2 ch), skip sc at base of 4 ch and next beaded ch, *1 hdc in next sc, ch 2, skip 1 beaded ch, rep from * to end, 1 slip st in 2nd of 4 ch at beg of round.

**Round 3** [1 slip st, 1 hdc, 2 dc, 1 hdc and 1 slip st] in each ch sp to end, 1 slip st in first slip st. 8 petals.
Fasten off.

Attach B to top of one hdc of round 2 and cont as foll:

**Round 4** Working behind petals of previous round: ch 1 (does NOT count as st), 1 sc in hdc where yarn was rejoined, *ch 2, 1 sc in next hdc of round 2 between petals; rep from * to end, replacing sc at end of last rep with 1 slip st in first sc.

**Round 5** Slip st in first ch sp, [ch 3, 1 dc, 1 hdc, 1 slip st, 1 hdc and 2 dc] in same ch sp, [2 dc, 1 hdc, 1 slip st, 1 hdc and 2 dc] in each ch sp to end, 1 slip st in top of 3 ch at beg of round. 8 petals.
Fasten off.

## Finishing

Do NOT press.

Using photograph as a guide, attach flowers to hair clips or hairbands.

# stripy snake

• • • • • • • • •

This stripy snake is great fun to crochet and great fun to play with, too! The pattern looks a bit intimidating because it is so long (in order to cover all the stripe instructions), but in fact it is very easy to crochet, as it is basically a long tube in lots of colors. You could make an even simpler version, if you wished, in just one color in single crochet, or perhaps with a few lines of stripes.

The pattern starts at the snake's tail and ends at his head; the tongue is then worked separately and stitched into the seam at the mouth.

Once your child is too old to play with it, it could make an excellent draft eliminator along the base of a door or window, if you crochet it to a suitable length!

## Size
Finished snake is 3in/8cm wide and 45¼in/115cm long, excluding tongue.

## Yarns
2 x 50g/1¾oz balls of Rowan *RYC Cashsoft DK* in **A** (Lime 509), and 1 ball in each of **B** (Ballad Blue 508), **C** (Glacier 504), **D** (Donkey 517), **E** (Mirage 503), **G** (Savannah 507), and **H** (Poppy 512)
1 x 50g/1¾oz ball of Rowan *RYC Cashsoft Baby DK* in **F** (Chicory 804)

## Hook
Size G-6 (4mm) crochet hook

## Extras
Washable toy filling
Scrap of white felt (for eyes)
Black sewing thread
2 small black buttons

## Gauge
18 sts and 20 rows to 4in/10cm measured over sc using size G-6 (4mm) hook *or size to obtain correct gauge.*

## Abbreviations
See page 117.

## To make
Using size G-6 (4mm) hook and B, ch 2.
**Round 1 (RS)** 5 sc in 2nd ch from hook, 1 slip st in first sc, turn. 5 sts.
**Round 2** Ch 1 (does NOT count as st), 1 sc in each sc to end, 1 slip st in first sc, turn.
**Rounds 3 and 4** As round 2.
**Round 5** Ch 1 (does NOT count as st), 2 sc in each sc to end, 1 slip st in first sc, turn. 10 sts.
**Rounds 6 to 11** As round 2.
**Round 12** Ch 1 (does NOT count as st), [1 sc in next sc, 2 sc in next sc] 5 times, 1 slip st in first sc, turn. 15 sts.
**Rounds 13 to 19** As round 2.
**Round 20** Ch 1 (does NOT count as st), [1 sc in each of next 2 sc, 2 sc in next sc] 5 times, 1 slip st in first sc, turn. 20 sts.
Joining in and breaking off colors as required, cont as foll:
**Rounds 21 to 27** Using A, ch 1 (does NOT count as st), 1 sc in each sc to end, 1 slip st in first sc, turn.
**Round 28** Using A, ch 1 (does NOT count as st), [1 sc in each of next 3 sc, 2 sc in next sc] 5 times, 1 slip st in first sc, turn. 25 sts.
**Round 29** Using B, ch 1 (does NOT count as st), *1 sc in next sc, ch 1, skip 1 sc, rep from * to last sc, 1 sc in last sc, 1 slip st in first sc, turn.
**Round 30** Using C, ch 1 (does NOT count as st), *1 sc in next sc, 1 sc in next ch sp, rep from * to last sc, 1 sc in last sc, 1 slip st in first sc, turn.
**Round 31** Using D, ch 1 (does NOT count as st), *1 sc in next sc, ch 1, skip 1 sc, rep from * to last sc, 1 sc in last sc, 1 slip st in first sc, turn.
**Round 32** Using E, ch 1 (does NOT count as st), *1 sc in next sc, 1 sc in next ch sp, rep from * to last sc, 1 sc in last sc, 1 slip st in first sc, turn.
**Rounds 33 to 35** Using E, ch 1 (does NOT count as st), 1 sc in each sc to end, 1 slip st in first sc, turn.
**Rounds 36 and 37** Using F, ch 1 (does NOT count as st), 1 sc in each sc to end, 1 slip st in first sc, turn.
**Round 38** Using F, ch 1 (does NOT count as st), [1 sc in each of next 4 sc, 2 sc in next sc] 5 times, 1 slip st in first sc, turn. 30 sts.
**Round 39** Using A, ch 1 (does NOT count as st), *1 sc in next sc, ch 1, skip 1 sc, rep from * to end, 1 slip st in first sc, turn.
**Round 40** Using F, ch 1 (does NOT count as st), *1 sc in next sc, 1 sc in next ch sp, rep from * to end, 1 slip st in

first sc, turn.

**Round 41** Using B, ch 1 (does NOT count as st), *1 sc in next sc, ch 1, skip 1 sc, rep from * to end, 1 slip st in first sc, turn.

**Round 42** Using C, ch 1 (does NOT count as st), *1 sc in next sc, 1 sc in next ch sp, rep from * to end, 1 slip st in first sc, turn.

**Round 43** Using D, ch 1 (does NOT count as st), *1 sc in next sc, ch 1, skip 1 sc, rep from * to end, 1 slip st in first sc, turn.

**Round 44** Using A, ch 1 (does NOT count as st), *1 sc in next sc, 1 sc in next ch sp, rep from * to end, 1 slip st in first sc, turn.

**Round 45** As round 43.

**Round 46** Using G, ch 1 (does NOT count as st), *1 sc in next sc, 1 sc in next ch sp, rep from * to end, 1 slip st in first sc, turn.

**Round 47** Using G, ch 1 (does NOT count as st), 1 sc in each sc to end, 1 slip st in first sc, turn.

**Round 48** Using G, ch 1 (does NOT count as st), [1 sc in each of next 5 sc, 2 sc in next sc] 5 times, 1 slip st in first sc, turn. 35 sts.

**Round 49** Using C, ch 1 (does NOT count as st), *1 sc in next sc, ch 1, skip 1 sc, rep from * to last sc, 1 sc in last sc, 1 slip st in first sc, turn.

**Round 50** Using G, ch 1 (does NOT count as st), *1 sc in next sc, 1 sc in next ch sp, rep from * to last sc, 1 sc in last sc, 1 slip st in first sc, turn.

**Rounds 51 to 58** Using A, ch 1 (does NOT count as st), 1 sc in each sc to end, 1 slip st in first sc, turn.

**Rounds 59 to 67** As rounds 29 to 37.

**Note:** You may find it easiest to insert the toy filling inside the snake as you go along, rather than attempting to insert it all once the snake is complete! If so, start now by inserting filling in tail section and then filling each new length as it is worked.

**Round 68** Using F, ch 1 (does NOT count as st), 1 sc in each sc to end, 1 slip st in first sc, turn.

**Round 69** Using A, ch 1 (does NOT count as st), *1 sc in next sc, ch 1, skip 1 sc, rep from * to last sc, 1 sc in last sc, 1 slip st in first sc, turn.

**Round 70** Using F, ch 1 (does NOT count as st), *1 sc in next sc, 1 sc in next ch sp, rep from * to last sc, 1 sc in last sc, 1 slip st in first sc, turn.

**Round 71** Using B, ch 1 (does NOT count as st), *1 sc in next sc, ch 1, skip 1 sc, rep from * to last sc, 1 sc in last sc, 1 slip st in first sc, turn.

*stripy snake*

**Round 72** Using C, ch 1 (does NOT count as st), *1 sc in next sc, 1 sc in next ch sp, rep from * to last sc, 1 sc in last sc, 1 slip st in first sc, turn.

**Round 73** Using D, ch 1 (does NOT count as st), *1 sc in next sc, ch 1, skip 1 sc, rep from * to last sc, 1 sc in last sc, 1 slip st in first sc, turn.

**Round 74** Using A, ch 1 (does NOT count as st), *1 sc in next sc, 1 sc in next ch sp, rep from * to last sc, 1 sc in last sc, 1 slip st in first sc, turn.

**Round 75** As round 43.

**Round 76** Using G, ch 1 (does NOT count as st), *1 sc in next sc, 1 sc in next ch sp, rep from * to last sc, 1 sc in last sc, 1 slip st in first sc, turn.

**Rounds 77 and 78** Using G, ch 1 (does NOT count as st), 1 sc in each sc to end, 1 slip st in first sc, turn.

**Round 79** Using C, ch 1 (does NOT count as st), *1 sc in next sc, ch 1, skip 1 sc, rep from * to last sc, 1 sc in last sc, 1 slip st in first sc, turn.

**Round 80** Using G, ch 1 (does NOT count as st), *1 sc in next sc, 1 sc in next ch sp, rep from * to last sc, 1 sc in last sc, 1 slip st in first sc, turn.

**Rounds 81 to 200** As rounds 51 to 80, 4 times.
Break off contrasts and cont using A only.

SHAPE HEAD

**Round 201** Ch 1 (does NOT count as st), 2 sc in sc at base of 1 ch, 1 sc in each sc to end, 1 slip st in first sc, turn. 36 sts.

**Round 202** Ch 1 (does NOT count as st), 1 sc in each st to end, 1 slip st in first sc, turn.

**Round 203** Ch 1 (does NOT count as st), [2 sc in next sc, 1 sc in each of next 7 sc, 2 sc in next sc] 4 times, 1 slip st in first sc, turn. 44 sts.

**Rounds 204 and 205** As round 202.

**Round 206** Ch 1 (does NOT count as st), 1 sc in each of next 10 sc, 2 sc in each of next 2 sc, 1 sc in each of next 20 sc, 2 sc in each of next 2 sc, 1 sc in each of last 10 sc, 1 slip st in first sc, turn. 48 sts.

**Round 207** Ch 1 (does NOT count as st), 2 sc in first sc, 1 sc in each of next 22 sc, 2 sc in each of next 2 sc, 1 sc in each of next 22 sc, 2 sc in last sc, 1 slip st in first sc, turn. 52 sts.

**Round 208** As round 202.

**Round 209** Ch 1 (does NOT count as st), 1 sc in each of next 12 sc, 2 sc in each of next 2 sc, 1 sc in each of next 24 sc, 2 sc in each of next 2 sc, 1 sc in each of last 12 sc, 1 slip st in first sc, turn. 56 sts.

**Rounds 210 to 212** As round 202.

**Round 213** Ch 1 (does NOT count as st), 1 sc in each of next 13 sc, 2 sc in each of next 2 sc, 1 sc in each of next 26 sc, 2 sc in each of next 2 sc, 1 sc in each of last 13 sc, 1 slip st in first sc, turn. 60 sts.

**Rounds 214 to 219** As round 202.
Insert toy filling so snake is quite firmly filled.

**Round 220** Ch 1 (does NOT count as st), 1 sc in each of next 13 sc, [sc2tog over next 2 sc] twice, 1 sc in each of next 26 sc, [sc2tog over next 2 sc] twice, 1 sc in each of last 13 sc, 1 slip st in first sc, turn. 56 sts.

**Round 221** As round 202.

**Round 222** Ch 1 (does NOT count as st), 1 sc in each of next 12 sc, [sc2tog over next 2 sc] twice, 1 sc in each of next 24 sc, [sc2tog over next 2 sc] twice, 1 sc in each of last 12 sc, 1 slip st in first sc, turn. 52 sts.

**Round 223** As round 202.

**Round 224** Ch 1 (does NOT count as st), 1 sc in each of next 11 sc, [sc2tog over next 2 sc] twice, 1 sc in each of next 22 sc, [sc2tog over next 2 sc] twice, 1 sc in each of last 11 sc, 1 slip st in first sc, turn. 48 sts.

**Round 225** Ch 1 (does NOT count as st), sc2tog over first 2 sc, 1 sc in each of next 20 sts, [sc2tog over next 2 sc] twice, 1 sc in each of next 20 sts, sc2tog over last 2 sc, 1 slip st in first sc2tog, turn. 44 sts.

**Round 226** Ch 1 (does NOT count as st), 1 sc in each of next 9 sts, [sc2tog over next 2 sc] twice, 1 sc in each of next

18 sts, [sc2tog over next 2 sc] twice, 1 sc in each of last 9 sts, 1 slip st in first sc, turn. 40 sts.

**Round 227** Ch 1 (does NOT count as st), 1 sc in each of next 8 sc, [sc2tog over next 2 sts) twice, 1 sc in each of next 16 sc, [sc2tog over next 2 sts] twice, 1 sc in each of last 8 sc, 1 slip st in first sc, turn. 36 sts.

**Round 228** Ch 1 (does NOT count as st), [sc2tog over next 2 sts, 1 sc in each of next 5 sc, sc2tog over next 2 sts] 4 times, 1 slip st in first sc2tog, turn. 28 sts.

Insert toy filling in head section.

**Round 229** Ch 1 (does NOT count as st), 1 sc in each of next 5 sts, [sc2tog over next 2 sts] twice, 1 sc in each of next 10 sts, [sc2tog over next 2 sts] twice, 1 sc in each of last 5 sts, 1 slip st in first sc, turn. 24 sts.

**Round 230** Ch 1 (does NOT count as st), [sc2tog over next 2 sts, 1 sc in each of next 2 sts, sc2tog over next 2 sts] 4 times, 1 slip st in first sc2tog, turn. 16 sts.

Fasten off.

**Finishing**

Do NOT press.

**TONGUE**

Using size G-6 (4mm) hook and H, ch 10.

**Row 1** 1 sc in 2nd ch from hook, 1 sc in each of next 3 ch, turn, ch 5, turn, 1 sc in 2nd ch from hook, 1 sc in each of next 3 ch, 1 sc in each of rem 5 ch.

Fasten off.

Using photograph as a guide, close top of last round of snake, enclosing tongue in seam. From felt, cut 2 oval shapes, each approximately ⅝in/1.5cm by ¾in/2cm for eyes. Using photograph as a guide, pin eyes to head, then attach a button through each eye, using black sewing thread.

# teddy scarf and hat

This little hat and pocketed scarf set is very easy to crochet if you opt for the simplest form shown here. The alternative version has its own teddy decorations (see page 37) that are stitched on afterward.

Crocheted in a simple stitch pattern, neither the scarf nor the hat requires any shaping, so they make an ideal first project for novices. You can finish off the hat with an optional toning tassel at each corner.

The little teddy motifs are not difficult to make either, but require a little more skill.

Both versions make a great gift for a young baby.

# teddy scarf

## To fit age, approximately

| 0–9 | 12–18 | months |
|-----|-------|--------|

### Finished measurements

**WIDTH**

| 5½ | 6½ | in |
|----|----|----|
| 14 | 17 | cm |

**LENGTH**

| 32 | 35½ | in |
|----|-----|----|
| 81 | 90 | cm |

## Yarns

2 x 50g/1¾oz balls of Rowan *Calmer* in **MC** (Powder Puff 482 or Calmer 463), and 1 ball in each of **A** (Calm 461) and **B** (Drift 460)

## Hook

Size H-8 (5mm) crochet hook

## Extras

Scrap of lightweight black yarn for embroidery

## Gauge

20 sts and 20 rows to 4in/10cm measured over patt using size H-8 (5mm) hook *or size to obtain correct gauge*.

## Abbreviations

See page 117.

## Scarf

Using size H-8 (5mm) hook and MC, ch 28 (34).
**Foundation row (RS)** Using MC, ch 1 (does NOT count as st), 1 sc in each ch to end, turn. 27 (33) sts.
Cont in patt as foll:
**Row 1** Using MC, ch 1 (does NOT count as st), 1 sc in each sc to end, turn.
**Rows 2 and 3** As row 1.
Join in A.
**Row 4** Using A, ch 1 (does NOT count as st), 1 sc in first sc, *ch 1, skip 1 sc, 1 sc in next sc, rep from * to end, turn.
**Row 5** Using A, ch 1 (does NOT count as st), 1 sc in first sc, *1 sc in next ch sp, 1 sc in next sc, rep from * to end, turn.
**Row 6** As row 1.
These 6 rows form patt.
Work in patt until scarf measures approximately 31½ (35)in/ 80 (89)cm, ending after patt row 3.
Fasten off.

## Pockets (make 2)

Using size H-8 (5mm) hook and MC, ch 28.
**Foundation row (RS)** Using MC, ch 1 (does NOT count as st), 1 sc in each ch to end, turn. 27 sts.
Cont in patt as foll:
**Row 1** Using MC, ch 1 (does NOT count as st), 1 sc in each sc to end, turn.
**Rows 2 and 3** As row 1.
Join in A.
**Row 4** Using A, ch 1 (does NOT count as st), 1 sc in first sc, *ch 1, skip 1 sc, 1 sc in next sc, rep from * to end, turn.
**Row 5** Using A, ch 1 (does NOT count as st), 1 sc in first sc, *1 sc in next ch sp, 1 sc in next sc, rep from * to end, turn.
**Row 6** As row 1.
These 6 rows form patt.
Work in patt for 21 (27) more rows, ending after patt row 3.
Fasten off.

## Finishing

Press lightly on WS following instructions on yarn label.
**POCKET EDGINGS** (both alike)
With RS facing, using size H-8 (5mm) hook and B, attach yarn to one corner of Pocket,

ch 1 (does NOT count as st), work 1 row of sc along one row-end edge. Fasten off.

Lay Pockets on ends of Scarf so that "raw" edges match and Pocket Edging forms opening edge of Pocket and sew in place.

### SCARF EDGING

With RS facing, using size H-8 (5mm) hook and B, attach yarn to outer edge of Scarf, ch 1 (does NOT count as st), work 1 round of sc around entire outer edge, working through both layers along sides of Pockets, working 3 sc in each corner point and ending with 1 slip st in first sc.

Fasten off.

### TEDDY FACES (make 2)

Using size H-8 (5mm) hook and A, ch 4 and join with a slip st to first ch to form a ring.

**Round 1 (RS)** Ch 1 (does NOT count as st), 8 sc in ring, 1 slip st in first sc, turn. 8 sts.

**Round 2** Ch 1 (does NOT count as st), *1 sc in next sc, ch 1, rep from * to end, 1 slip st in first sc, turn. 16 sts.

**Round 3** Ch 1 (does NOT count as st), *1 sc in next ch sp, 1 sc in next sc, rep from * to end, 1 slip st in first sc, turn.

**Rounds 4 and 5** As rounds 2 and 3. 32 sts.

**Round 6** Ch 1 (does NOT count as st), 1 sc in each sc to end, 1 slip st in first sc, turn.

Fasten off.

**TEDDY EARS** (make 4)

Work as given for Teddy Faces to end of round 2. 16 sts.

Break off A and join in B.

**Round 3** Ch 1 (does NOT count as st), 1 sc in first ch sp,
[1 sc in next sc, 1 sc in next ch sp] 6 times.

Fasten off.

**TEDDY MUZZLE** (make 2)

Using B, work as given for Teddy Faces to end of round 3.
16 sts.

Fasten off.

Using photograph as a guide, sew Muzzle onto Face, then
Ears to outer edge of Face. Using black yarn, embroider chain
stitch nose and backstitch mouth onto Muzzle. Using black
yarn, embroider chain stitch eyes and backstitch eyebrows
onto Face. Using B, embroider one big lazy daisy stitch onto
each eye. Sew completed Teddy Face to Pocket.

# teddy hat

## To fit age, approximately

| 0–3 | 6–9 | 12–18 | months |
|-----|-----|-------|--------|

### Finished measurements

#### CIRCUMFERENCE AROUND HEAD

| 13¼ | 15½ | 18 | in |
|-----|-----|-----|-----|
| 34 | 40 | 46 | cm |

## Yarns

1 x 50g/1¾oz ball of Rowan *Calmer* in each of **MC** (Powder
Puff 482 or Calmer 463), **A** (Calm 461) and **B** (Drift 460)

## Hook

Size H-8 (5mm) crochet hook

## Extras

Scrap of lightweight black yarn for embroidery

## Gauge

20 sts and 20 rows to 4in/10cm measured over patt using
size H-8 (5mm) hook *or size to obtain correct gauge.*

## Abbreviations

See page 117.

## Main section

Using size H-8 (5mm) hook and MC, ch 48 (52: 56).

**Foundation row (RS)** Using MC, ch 1 (does NOT count as st),
1 sc in each ch to end, turn. 47 (51: 55) sts.

Cont in patt as foll:

**Row 1** Using MC, ch 1 (does NOT count as st), 1 sc in each sc
to end, turn.

**Rows 2 and 3** As row 1.

Join in A.

**Row 4** Using A, ch 1 (does NOT count as st), 1 sc in first
sc, *ch 1, skip 1 sc, 1 sc in next sc, rep from * to end,
turn.

**Row 5** Using A, ch 1 (does NOT count as st), 1 sc in first sc,
*1 sc in next ch sp, 1 sc in next sc, rep from * to end, turn.

**Row 6** As row 1.

These 6 rows form patt.

Work in patt for 27 (33: 39) rows more, ending after patt row
3—work should measure 6½ (7¾: 9)in /17 (20: 23)cm.

Fasten off.

## Lower band

Fold main section in half centrally along rows and join
foundation ch and last row edges. (Stripes should be at right
angles to fold.)

With RS facing, using size H-8 (5mm) hook and MC, attach
yarn at base of one seam and cont as foll:

**Round 1 (RS)** Ch 1 (does NOT count as st), 34 (40: 46) sc
along first row-end edge to other seam, 34 (40: 46) sc along
other row-end edge, 1 slip st in first sc, turn.

68 (80: 92) sts.

Join in A.

**Round 2** Using A, ch 1 (does NOT count as st), 1 sc in each sc to end, 1 slip st in first sc, turn.

**Round 3** Using MC, ch 1 (does NOT count as st), 1 sc in each sc to end, 1 slip st in first sc, turn.

**Round 4** As round 2.

Join in B.

**Round 5** Using B, ch 1 (does NOT count as st), 1 sc in each sc to end, 1 slip st in first sc.

Fasten off.

### Finishing

Press lightly on WS following instructions on yarn label.

Make one Teddy Face, one Teddy Muzzle and two Teddy Ears as given for Scarf. Following instructions as given for Scarf, assemble Teddy Face and attach to front of Hat.

Using B, make two 2¼in/6cm tassels and attach to corners of Hat.

# bootees

● ● ● ● ● ● ● ● ●

Here come the teddies again, this time adorning the fronts of little teddy bootees and making a wonderful gift for a tiny baby! But they are just as useful for an older baby who is taking his or her first steps, because— crocheted in Rowan *Calmer*—they are sturdy as well as soft. The teddy faces are an optional extra, so you can make the basic bootees if you prefer.

Any mom would be thrilled to get these, especially with the little card on page 109 and wrapped up in tissue in the beribboned box on page 110. Make them in blue for a boy or pink for a girl, if you want to follow tradition.

**To fit age, approximately**

| 0–9 | 12–18 | months |
|-----|-------|--------|

**Finished measurements**

LENGTH OF FOOT

| 4 | 4½ | in |
|-----|-----|-----|
| 10 | 11 | cm |

**Yarns**

1 x 50g/1¾oz ball of Rowan *Calmer* in each of **MC** (Powder Puff 482 or Calmer 463), **A** (Calm 461) and **B** (Drift 460)

**Hook**

Size H-8 (5mm) crochet hook

**Extras**

Scrap of lightweight black yarn for embroidery

**Gauge**

20 sts and 20 rows to 4in/10cm measured over sc using size H-8 (5mm) hook *or size to obtain correct gauge.*

**Abbreviations**

See page 117.

**Bootees** (both alike)

Using size H-8 (5mm) hook and MC, ch 24 (28) and join with a slip st to first ch to form a ring.

**Foundation round (RS)** Ch 1 (does NOT count as st), 1 sc in each ch to end, 1 slip st in first sc, turn. 24 (28) sts.

Cont in patt as foll:

**Round 1** Ch 1 (does NOT count as st), 1 sc in each sc to end, 1 slip st in first sc, turn.

This round forms sc fabric.

Work in sc for 8 (10) rounds more, ending with RS facing for next round.

Do NOT fasten off.

SHAPE INSTEP

Using size H-8 (5mm) hook and separate length of MC, skip first 9 (11) sts of next round, rejoin yarn to next sc, ch 1 (does NOT count as st), 1 sc in st where yarn was rejoined, 1 sc in each of next 5 (6) sc and turn.

Work on these 6 (7) sts only for instep.

**Next row (WS)** Ch 1 (does NOT count as st), 1 sc in each sc to end, turn.

Rep this row 8 (9) times more.

**Next row** Ch 1 (does NOT count as st), sc2tog over first 2 sc, 1 sc in each of next 2 (3) sc, sc2tog over last 2 sc, turn. 4 (5) sts.

**Next row** Ch 1 (does NOT count as st), sc2tog over first 2 sts, 1 sc in next 0 (1) sc, sc2tog over last 2 sts. 2 (3) sts.

Fasten off.

Return to last complete round worked and cont as foll:

**Next round (RS)** Ch 1 (does NOT count as st), 1 sc in each of first 9 (11) sc, 1 sc in each of next 12 (13) row-ends down first side of instep, 1 sc in each of next 2 (3) sts across end of instep, 1 sc in each of next 12 (13) row-ends up other side of instep, 1 sc in each of last 9 (10) sc of last complete round, 1 slip st in first sc, turn. 44 (50) sts.

Work in sc for 5 (7) rounds, ending with RS facing for next round.

SHAPE SOLE

**Round 1 (RS)** Ch 1 (does NOT count as st), 1 sc in each of first 3 (4) sc, sc2tog over next 2 sc, 1 sc in each of next 12 (14) sc, sc2tog over next 2 sc, 1 sc in each of next 6 (7) sc, sc2tog over next 2 sc, 1 sc in each of next 12 (14) sc, sc2tog over next 2 sc, 1 sc in each of last 3 sc, 1 slip st in first sc, turn. 40 (46) sts.

**Round 2** Ch 1 (does NOT count as st), 1 sc in each of first 2 sc, sc2tog over next 2 sc, 1 sc in each of next 12 (14) sc, sc2tog over next 2 sc, 1 sc in each of next 4 (5) sc, sc2tog over next 2 sc, 1 sc in each of next 12 (14) sc, sc2tog over next 2 sc, 1 sc in each of last 2 (3) sc, 1 slip st in first sc, turn. 36 (42) sts.

**Round 3** Ch 1 (does NOT count as st), 1 sc in each of first
1 (2) sc, sc2tog over next 2 sc, 1 sc in each of next 12 (14)
sc, sc2tog over next 2 sc, 1 sc in each of next 2 (3) sc,
sc2tog over next 2 sc, 1 sc in each of next 12 (14) sc, sc2tog
over next 2 sc, 1 sc in last sc, 1 slip st in first sc, turn.
32 (38) sts.

**Round 4** Ch 1 (does NOT count as st), sc2tog over first 2 sc,
1 sc in each of next 12 (14) sc, sc2tog over next 2 sc, 1 sc in
each of next 0 (1) sc, sc2tog over next 2 sc, 1 sc in each of
next 12 (14) sc, sc2tog over next 2 sc, 1 sc in each of last 0
(1) sc, 1 slip st in first sc. 28 (34) sts.
Fasten off.

## Finishing

Do NOT press.
Fold first 4 rounds to RS to form turn-back cuff.

### EDGING

With RS of turn-back facing, using size H-8 (5mm) hook and
B, attach yarn to foundation ch edge at center back of
Bootee, ch 1 (does NOT count as st), work 1 round of sc
around foundation ch edge, ending with 1 slip st in first sc.
Fasten off.

### TEDDY FACES (make 2)

Using size H-8 (5mm) hook and A, ch 3 and join with a slip
st to first ch to form a ring.

**Round 1 (RS)** Ch 1 (does NOT count as st), 6 sc in ring, 1 slip
st in first sc, turn. 6 sts.

**Round 2** Ch 1 (does NOT count as st), *1 sc in next sc, ch 1,
rep from * to end, 1 slip st in first sc, turn. 12 sts.

**Round 3** Ch 1 (does NOT count as st), *1 sc in next ch sp,
1 sc in next sc, rep from * to end, 1 slip st in first sc, turn.

**Rounds 4 and 5** As rounds 2 and 3. 24 sts.

**Round 6** Ch 1 (does NOT count as st), 1 sc in each sc to end,
1 slip st in first sc.
Fasten off.

### TEDDY EARS (make 4)

Work as given for Teddy Faces to end of round 2. 12 sts.
Break off A and join in B.

**Round 3** Ch 1 (does NOT count as st), 1 sc in first ch sp, [1 sc
in next sc, 1 sc in next ch sp] 4 times, 1 sc in next sc.
Fasten off.

### TEDDY MUZZLE (make 2)

Using B, work as given for Teddy Faces to end of round 3.
12 sts.
Fasten off.

Using photograph as a guide, sew Muzzle to Face, then Ears
to outer edge of Face. Using black yarn, embroider chain
stitch nose, and backstitch mouth onto Muzzle. Using black
yarn, embroider chain stitch eyes and backstitch eyebrows
onto Face. Using B, embroider one big lazy daisy stitch onto
each eye. Sew completed Teddy Face onto front of Bootee.

# his and hers teddies

• • • • • • • • • •

What child would not love this funny little teddy with his squashy, flexible body and almost clownlike face? Make a girl's or a boy's version in pink or blue or, if you wish, a more traditionally unisex version in brown. Crocheted in Rowan's *Cashsoft*, they are lovely and soft to the touch, too.

These little toys take a bit more patience than some of the simpler projects in the book because there are several pieces to make and stitch together, but they are ideal for an intermediate crocheter.

## Size
Finished teddy sits 7¾in/20cm tall,
excluding ears.

## Yarns
2 x 50g/1¾oz balls of Rowan *RYC Cashsoft Baby
DK* in **A** (Pixie 807 or Cloud 805)
1 x 50g/1¾oz ball of Rowan *RYC Cashsoft DK* in
each of **B** (Cream 500) and **C** (Savannah 507)

## Hook
Size D-3 (3mm) crochet hook

## Extras
Washable toy filling
Dried beans (optional)
Scrap of brown yarn for embroidery

## Gauge
20 sts and 22 rows to 4in/10cm measured over
sc using size D-3 (3mm) hook *or size to obtain
correct gauge.*

## Abbreviations
See page 117.

## Safety note
Dried beans have been added into toy filling
to give the toy extra weight so that it sits well
and the legs and arms hang properly. If toy
is to be given to a baby or very young child,
these beans could work their way through the
crochet and there could be a risk of the child
choking on them. To avoid this, enclose beans
inside a tiny little fabric bag that is securely
sewn closed.

## Body and head

Using size D-3 (3mm) hook and A, ch 11.

**Round 1 (RS)** 2 sc in 2nd ch from hook, 1 sc in each of next 8 ch, 4 sc in last ch, working back along other side of foundation ch: 1 sc in each of next 8 ch, 2 sc in same ch as used for 2 sc at beg of round, 1 slip st in first sc, turn. 24 sts.

**Round 2** Ch 1 (does NOT count as st), 2 sc in first sc, [1 sc in each of next 4 sc, 2 sc in each of next 2 sc] 3 times, 1 sc in each of next 4 sc, 2 sc in last sc, 1 slip st in first sc, turn. 32 sts.

**Round 3** Ch 1 (does NOT count as st), 2 sc in first sc, [1 sc in each of next 6 sc, 2 sc in each of next 2 sc] 3 times, 1 sc in each of next 6 sc, 2 sc in last sc, 1 slip st in first sc, turn. 40 sts.

**Round 4** Ch 1 (does NOT count as st), 2 sc in first sc, 1 sc in each of next 18 sc, 2 sc in each of next 2 sc, 1 sc in each of next 18 sc, 2 sc in last sc, 1 slip st in first sc, turn. 44 sts.

**Round 5** Ch 1 (does NOT count as st), 1 sc in each sc to end, 1 slip st in first sc, turn.

**Round 6** Ch 1 (does NOT count as st), 2 sc in first sc, 1 sc in each of next 20 sc, 2 sc in each of next 2 sc, 1 sc in each of next 20 sc, 2 sc in last sc, 1 slip st in first sc, turn. 48 sts. Join in B.

**Round 7** Using A ch 1 (does NOT count as st), 1 sc in each of first 8 sc, using B 1 sc in each of next 8 sc, using A 1 sc in each of last 32 sc, 1 slip st in first sc, turn.

**Round 8** Using A ch 1 (does NOT count as st), 1 sc in each of first 31 sc, using B 1 sc in each of next 10 sc, using A 1 sc in each of last 7 sc, 1 slip st in first sc, turn.

**Round 9** Using A ch 1 (does NOT count as st), 1 sc in each of first 6 sc, using B 1 sc in each of next 12 sc, using A 1 sc in each of last 30 sc, 1 slip st in first sc, turn.

**Round 10** Using A ch 1 (does NOT count as st), 1 sc in each of first 29 sc, using B 1 sc in each of next 14 sc, using A 1 sc in each of last 5 sc, 1 slip st in first sc, turn.

**Round 11** Using A ch 1 (does NOT count as st), 1 sc in each of first 5 sc, using B 1 sc in each of next 14 sc, using A 1 sc in each of last 29 sc, 1 slip st in first sc, turn.

**Rounds 12 and 13** As rounds 10 and 11.

**Round 14** As round 10.

**Round 15** Using A ch 1 (does NOT count as st), sc2tog over first 2 sc, 1 sc in each of next 4 sc, using B 1 sc in each of next 12 sc, using A 1 sc in each of next 4 sc, [sc2tog over next 2 sc] twice, 1 sc in each of next 20 sc, sc2tog over last 2 sc, 1 slip st in first sc2tog, turn. 44 sts.

**Round 16** Using A ch 1 (does NOT count as st), 1 sc in each of first 27 sc, using B 1 sc in each of next 12 sc, using A 1 sc in each of last 5 sc, 1 slip st in first sc, turn.

**Round 17** Using A ch 1 (does NOT count as st), 1 sc in each of first 5 sc, using B 1 sc in each of next 12 sc, using A 1 sc in each of last 27 sc, 1 slip st in first sc, turn.

**Round 18** Using A ch 1 (does NOT count as st), sc2tog over first 2 sc, 1 sc in each of next 18 sc, [sc2tog over next 2 sc] twice, 1 sc in each of next 4 sc, using B 1 sc in each of next 10 sc, using A 1 sc in each of next 4 sc, sc2tog over last 2 sc, 1 slip st in first sc2tog, turn. 40 sts.

**Round 19** Using A ch 1 (does NOT count as st), 1 sc in each of first 5 sc, using B 1 sc in each of next 10 sc, using A 1 sc in each of last 25 sc, 1 slip st in first sc, turn.

**Round 20** Using A ch 1 (does NOT count as st), sc2tog over first 2 sc, 1 sc in each of next 16 sc, [sc2tog over next 2 sc] twice, 1 sc in each of next 4 sc, using B 1 sc in each of next 8 sc, using A 1 sc in each of next 4 sc, sc2tog over last 2 sc, 1 slip st in first sc2tog, turn. 36 sts.

**Round 21** Using A ch 1 (does NOT count as st), 1 sc in each of first 5 sc, using B 1 sc in each of next 8 sc, using A 1 sc in each of last 23 sc, 1 slip st in first sc, turn.

**Round 22** Using A ch 1 (does NOT count as st), sc2tog over first 2 sc, 1 sc in each of next 14 sc, [sc2tog over next 2 sc] twice, 1 sc in each of next 4 sc, using B 1 sc in each of next 6 sc, using A 1 sc in each of next 4 sc, sc2tog over last 2 sc, 1 slip st in first sc2tog, turn. 32 sts.

**Round 23** Using A ch 1 (does NOT count as st), 1 sc in each of first 5 sc, using B 1 sc in each of next 6 sc, using A 1 sc in each of last 21 sc, 1 slip st in first sc, turn.

**Round 24** Using A ch 1 (does NOT count as st), sc2tog over first 2 sc, 1 sc in each of next 12 sc, [sc2tog over next 2 sc] twice, 1 sc in each of next 4 sc, using B 1 sc in each of next 4 sc, using A 1 sc in each of next 4 sc, sc2tog over last 2 sc, 1 slip st in first sc2tog, turn. 28 sts.

Break off B and cont using A only.

**Round 25** As round 5.

**Round 26** Ch 1 (does NOT count as st), sc2tog over first 2 sc, 1 sc in each of next 10 sc, [sc2tog over next 2 sc] twice, 1 sc in each of next 10 sc, sc2tog over last 2 sc, 1 slip st in first sc2tog, turn. 24 sts.

**Round 27** As round 5.

**Round 28** Ch 1 (does NOT count as st), sc2tog over first 2 sc, 1 sc in each of next 8 sc, [sc2tog over next 2 sc] twice, 1 sc in each of next 8 sc, sc2tog over last 2 sc, 1 slip st in first sc2tog, turn. 20 sts.

Insert a little toy filling in Body section, add a handful of dried peas or beans (to add weight), then add more toy filling so that Body section is quite firmly filled.

**SHAPE NECK**

**Round 29** Ch 1 (does NOT count as st), [sc2tog over next 2 sc, 1 sc in next sc, sc2tog over next 2 sc] 4 times, 1 slip st in first sc2tog, turn. 12 sts.

**Round 30** As round 5.

**Round 31** Ch 1 (does NOT count as st), [2 sc in next sc, 1 sc in next sc, 2 sc in next sc] 4 times, 1 slip st in first sc, turn. 20 sts.

Insert a little more toy filling in neck if required.

**SHAPE HEAD**

**Round 32** Ch 1 (does NOT count as st), 2 sc in first sc, 1 sc in each of next 8 sc, [2 sc in each of next 2 sc, 1 sc in each of next 3 sc] twice, 2 sc in last sc, 1 slip st in first sc, turn. 26 sts.

**Round 33** Ch 1 (does NOT count as st), 2 sc in first sc, [1 sc in each of next 5 sc, 2 sc in each of next 2 sc] twice, 1 sc in each of next 10 sc, 2 sc in last sc, 1 slip st in first sc, turn. 32 sts.

**Round 34** As round 5.

**Round 35** Ch 1 (does NOT count as st), 2 sc in first sc, [1 sc in each of next 7 sc, 2 sc in each of next 2 sc] twice, 1 sc in each of next 12 sc, 2 sc in last sc, 1 slip st in first sc, turn. 38 sts.

**Rounds 36 to 43** As round 5.

**Round 44** Ch 1 (does NOT count as st), sc2tog over first 2 sc, 1 sc in each of next 12 sc, [sc2tog over next 2 sc] twice, 1 sc in each of next 18 sc, sc2tog over last 2 sc, 1 slip st in first sc2tog, turn. 34 sts.

**Round 45** Ch 1 (does NOT count as st), 1 sc in each of first 8 sc, [sc2tog over next 2 sc] twice, 1 sc in each of last 22 sc, 1 slip st in first sc, turn. 32 sts.

**Round 46** Ch 1 (does NOT count as st), sc2tog over first 2 sc, 1 sc in each of next 10 sc, [sc2tog over next 2 sc] twice, 1 sc in each of next 14 sc, sc2tog over last 2 sc, 1 slip st in first sc2tog, turn. 28 sts.

**Round 47** Ch 1 (does NOT count as st), sc2tog over first 2 sc, 1 sc in each of next 4 sc, [sc2tog over next 2 sc] twice, 1 sc in each of next 4 sc, [sc2tog over next 2 sc] twice, 1 sc in each of next 8 sc, sc2tog over last 2 sc, 1 slip st in first sc2tog, turn. 22 sts.

**Round 48** Ch 1 (does NOT count as st), sc2tog over first 2 sc, 1 sc in each of next 6 sc, [sc2tog over next 2 sc] twice, 1 sc in each of next 2 sc, [sc2tog over next 2 sc] twice, 1 sc in each of next 2 sc, sc2tog over last 2 sc, 1 slip st in first sc2tog, turn. 16 sts.

Insert toy filling in Head section so that Head is firmly filled.

**Round 49** Ch 1 (does NOT count as st), [sc2tog over next 2 sc] 8 times, 1 slip st in first sc2tog, turn. 8 sts.

**Round 50** Ch 1 (does NOT count as st), [sc2tog over next 2 sc] 4 times, 1 slip st in first sc2tog. 4 sts.

Fasten off, leaving a fairly long end. Insert a little more toy filling if required then run a gathering thread around top of last round. Pull up tight and fasten off securely.

## Muzzle

Using size D-3 (3mm) hook and B, ch 2.

**Round 1** (RS) 6 sc in 2nd ch from hook, 1 slip st in first sc, turn. 6 sts.

**Round 2** Ch 1 (does NOT count as st), 2 sc in first sc, 1 sc in next sc, 2 sc in each of next 2 sc, 1 sc in next sc, 2 sc in last sc, 1 slip st in first sc, turn. 10 sts.

**Round 3** Ch 1 (does NOT count as st), 1 sc in each sc to end, 1 slip st in first sc, turn.

**Round 4** Ch 1 (does NOT count as st), 1 sc in first sc, 2 sc in next sc, 3 sc in next sc, 2 sc in next sc, 1 sc in each of next 2 sc, 2 sc in next sc, 3 sc in next sc, 2 sc in next sc, 1 sc in last sc, 1 slip st in first sc, turn. 18 sts.

**Round 5** As round 3.

**Round 6** Ch 1 (does NOT count as st), 1 sc in each of first 2 sc, 2 sc in next sc, 1 sc in each of next 3 sc, 2 sc in next sc, 1 sc in each of next 4 sc, 2 sc in next sc, 1 sc in each of next 3 sc, 2 sc in next sc, 1 sc in each of last 2 sc, 1 slip st in first sc, turn. 22 sts.

**Round 7** As round 3.

**Round 8** Ch 1 (does NOT count as st), [1 sc in each of next 3 sc, 2 sc in next sc] twice, 1 sc in each of next 6 sc, [2 sc in next sc, 1 sc in each of next 3 sc] twice, 1 slip st in first sc, turn. 26 sts.

**Round 9** As round 3.

**Round 10** Ch 1 (does NOT count as st), 1 sc in each of first 5 sc, 2 sc in next sc, 1 sc in next sc, 2 sc in next sc, 1 sc in each of next 10 sc, 2 sc in next sc, 1 sc in next sc, 2 sc in next sc, 1 sc in each of last 5 sc, 1 slip st in first sc, turn. 30 sts.

**Rounds 11 to 14** As round 3.

Fasten off, leaving a long end. Insert toy filling inside

Muzzle, then sew top of last round to front of Head as in photograph positioning start and end of rounds under chin.

## Arms (make 2)

Using size D-3 (3mm) hook and B, ch 3.

**Round 1 (RS)** 2 sc in 2nd ch from hook, 4 sc in last ch, working back along other side of foundation ch: 2 sc in same ch as used for 2 sc at beg of round, 1 slip st in first sc, turn. 8 sts.

**Round 2** Ch 1 (does NOT count as st), 2 sc in first sc, 1 sc in each of next 2 sc, 2 sc in each of next 2 sc, 1 sc in each of next 2 sc, 2 sc in last sc, 1 slip st in first sc, turn. 12 sts.

**Round 3** Ch 1 (does NOT count as st), 1 sc in first sc, [2 sc in next sc, 1 sc in each of next 2 sc] 3 times, 2 sc in next sc, 1 sc in last sc, 1 slip st in first sc, turn. 16 sts.

Break off B and join in A.

**Round 4** Ch 1 (does NOT count as st), 1 sc in first sc, 2 sc in next sc, 1 sc in each of next 4 sc, 2 sc in next sc, 1 sc in each of next 2 sc, 2 sc in next sc, 1 sc in each of next 4 sc, 2 sc in next sc, 1 sc in last sc, 1 slip st in first sc, turn. 20 sts.

**Round 5** Ch 1 (does NOT count as st), 1 sc in each sc to end, 1 slip st in first sc, turn.

**Round 6** As round 5.

**Round 7** Ch 1 (does NOT count as st), 2 sc in first sc, 1 sc in each of next 5 sc, [sc2tog over next 2 sc] 4 times, 1 sc in each of next 5 sc, 2 sc in last sc, 1 slip st in first sc, turn. 18 sts.

**Round 8** Ch 1 (does NOT count as st), 2 sc in first sc, 1 sc in each of next 6 sc, [sc2tog over next 2 sc] twice, 1 sc in each of next 6 sc, 2 sc in last sc, 1 slip st in first sc, turn. 18 sts.

**Rounds 9 to 15** As round 8.

Now working in rows, not rounds, cont as foll:

**Row 16** Ch 1 (does NOT count as st), sc2tog over first 2 sc, 1 sc in each of next 5 sc, [sc2tog over next 2 sc] twice, 1 sc in each of next 5 sc, sc2tog over last 2 sc, turn. 14 sts.

**Row 17** Ch 1 (does NOT count as st), sc2tog over first 2 sc, 1 sc in each of next 3 sc, [sc2tog over next 2 sc] twice, 1 sc in each of next 3 sc, sc2tog over last 2 sc, turn. 10 sts.

**Row 18** Ch 1 (does NOT count as st), sc2tog over first 2 sc, 1 sc in next sc, [sc2tog over next 2 sc] twice, 1 sc in next sc, sc2tog over last 2 sc, turn. 6 sts.

**Row 19** Ch 1 (does NOT count as st), sc2tog over first 2 sc, 1 sc in each of next 2 sc, sc2tog over last 2 sc, turn. 4 sts.

**Row 20** Ch 1 (does NOT count as st), [sc2tog over next 2 sc] twice. 2 sts.

Fasten off.

Insert toy filling in hand section, adding a few dried peas or beans (to add weight), so that hand is firmly filled. Then insert toy filling in arm section so that it is soft and very lightly filled. Fold top of Arm flat and sew row-end edges closed. Sew Arm to side of Body as in photograph.

**Legs** (make 2)

Using size D-3 (3mm) hook and B, ch 5.

**Round 1 (RS)** 1 sc in 2nd ch from hook, 1 sc in each of next 2 ch, 2 sc in last ch, working back along other side of foundation ch: 1 sc in each of next 2 ch, 1 sc in same ch as used for sc at beg of round, 1 slip st in first sc, turn. 8 sts.

**Round 2** Ch 1 (does NOT count as st), 2 sc in first sc, 1 sc in each of next 2 sc, 2 sc in each of next 2 sc, 1 sc in each of next 2 sc, 2 sc in last sc, 1 slip st in first sc, turn. 12 sts.

**Round 3** Ch 1 (does NOT count as st), 2 sc in each of first 2 sc, 1 sc in each of next 2 sc, 2 sc in each of next 4 sc, 1 sc in each of next 2 sc, 2 sc in each of last 2 sc, 1 slip st in first sc, turn. 20 sts.

**Round 4** Ch 1 (does NOT count as st), 2 sc in first sc, 1 sc in next sc, 2 sc in next sc, 1 sc in each of next 4 sc, 2 sc in next sc, 1 sc in next sc, 2 sc in each of next 2 sc, 1 sc in next sc, 2 sc in next sc, 1 sc in each of next 4 sc, 2 sc in next sc, 1 sc in next sc, 2 sc in last sc, 1 slip st in first sc, turn. 28 sts.

**Round 5** Ch 1 (does NOT count as st), 1 sc in each of first

12 sc, 2 sc in next sc, 1 sc in each of next 2 sc, 2 sc in next sc, 1 sc in each of last 12 sc, 1 slip st in first sc, turn. 30 sts.

Break off B and join in A.

**Round 6** Ch 1 (does NOT count as st), 1 sc in each sc to end, 1 slip st in first sc, turn.

**Round 7** As round 6.

**Round 8** Ch 1 (does NOT count as st), 1 sc in each of first 13 sc, [sc2tog over next 2 sc] twice, 1 sc in each of last

13 sc, 1 slip st in first sc, turn. 28 sts.

**Round 9** Ch 1 (does NOT count as st), 2 sc in first sc, 1 sc in each of next 9 sc, [sc2tog over next 2 sc] 4 times, 1 sc in each of next 9 sc, 2 sc in last sc, 1 slip st in first sc, turn. 26 sts.

**Round 10** Ch 1 (does NOT count as st), 1 sc in each of first 9 sc, [sc2tog over next 2 sc] 4 times, 1 sc in each of last 9 sc, 1 slip st in first sc, turn. 22 sts.

**Round 11** Ch 1 (does NOT count as st), 1 sc in each of first 7 sc, [sc2tog over next 2 sc] 4 times, 1 sc in each of last 7 sc, 1 slip st in first sc, turn. 18 sts.

**Round 12** Ch 1 (does NOT count as st), 1 sc in each of first 7 sc, [sc2tog over next 2 sc] twice, 1 sc in each of last 7 sc, 1 slip st in first sc, turn. 16 sts.

**Round 13** As round 6.

**Round 14** Ch 1 (does NOT count as st), 2 sc in first sc, 1 sc in each of next 5 sc, [sc2tog over next 2 sc] twice, 1 sc in each of next 5 sc, 2 sc in last sc, 1 slip st in first sc, turn. 16 sts.

**Rounds 15 and 16** As round 6.

**Round 17** As round 14.

**Round 18** As round 6.

**Round 19** Ch 1 (does NOT count as st), 2 sc in first sc, 1 sc in each of next 14 sc, 2 sc in last sc, 1 slip st in first sc, turn. 18 sts.

**Round 20** Ch 1 (does NOT count as st), 1 sc in each of first 7 sc, [sc2tog over next 2 sc] twice, 1 sc in each of last 7 sc, 1 slip st in first sc, turn. 16 sts.

**Round 21** As round 19.

**Round 22** As round 6.

Now working in rows, not rounds, cont as foll:

**Row 23** Ch 1 (does NOT count as st), 1 sc in each of first 7 sc, [sc2tog over next 2 sc] twice, 1 sc in each of last 7 sc, turn. 16 sts.

**Row 24** Ch 1 (does NOT count as st), sc2tog over first 2 sc, 1 sc in each of next 12 sc, sc2tog over last 2 sc, turn. 14 sts.

**Row 25** Ch 1 (does NOT count as st), 1 sc in each of first

5 sc, [sc2tog over next 2 sc] twice, 1 sc in each of last 5 sc, turn. 12 sts.

**Row 26** Ch 1 (does NOT count as st), sc2tog over first 2 sc, 1 sc in each of next 8 sc, sc2tog over last 2 sc, turn. 10 sts.

**Row 27** Ch 1 (does NOT count as st), 1 sc in each of first 3 sc, [sc2tog over next 2 sc] twice, 1 sc in each of last 3 sc, turn. 8 sts.

**Row 28** Ch 1 (does NOT count as st), [sc2tog over next 2 sc] 4 times, turn. 4 sts.

**Row 29** Ch 1 (does NOT count as st), [sc2tog over next 2 sc] twice. 2 sts.

Fasten off.

Insert toy filling in foot section, adding a few dried beans (to add weight), so that foot is firmly filled. Then insert toy filling in leg section so that it is soft and very lightly filled. Fold top of Leg flat and sew row-end edges closed. Sew Leg to side of Body as in photograph.

## Finishing

Do NOT press.

EARS (make 2)

Using size D-3 (3mm) hook and A, ch 4.

**Round 1 (RS)** 1 sc in 2nd ch from hook, 1 sc in next ch, 2 sc in last ch, working back along other side of foundation ch: 1 sc in next ch, 1 sc in same ch as used for sc at beg of round, 1 slip st in first sc, turn. 6 sts.

**Round 2** Ch 1 (does NOT count as st), 2 sc in first sc, 1 sc in next sc, 2 sc in each of next 2 sc, 1 sc in next sc, 2 sc in last sc, 1 slip st in first sc, turn. 10 sts.

Join in C.

**Round 3** Using A ch 1 (does NOT count as st), 2 sc in first sc, 1 sc in next sc, using C 1 sc in next sc, using A 1 sc in next sc, 2 sc in each of next 2 sc, 1 sc in each of next 3 sc, 2 sc in last sc, 1 slip st in first sc, turn. 14 sts.

**Round 4** Using A ch 1 (does NOT count as st), 1 sc in each of first 9 sc, using C 1 sc in each of next 3 sc, using A 1 sc in each of last 2 sc, 1 slip st in first sc, turn.

**Round 5** Using A ch 1 (does NOT count as st), 1 sc in each of first 2 sc, using C 1 sc in each of next 3 sc, using A 1 sc in each of last 9 sc, 1 slip st in first sc, turn.

**Round 6** As round 4.

Fasten off.

Fold Ear flat, so that section in C is centrally placed on one side, then sew Ear to Head as in photograph.

**NOSE**

Using size D-3 (3mm) hook and C, ch 2.

**Round 1 (RS)** 4 sc in 2nd ch from hook, 1 slip st in first sc, turn. 4 sts.

**Round 2** Ch 1 (does NOT count as st), 2 sc in each sc to end, 1 slip st in first sc, turn. 8 sts.

**Round 3** Ch 1 (does NOT count as st), 1 sc in each sc to end, 1 slip st in first sc, turn.

**Round 4** As round 3.

Fasten off.

Insert a tiny amount of toy filling inside Nose, then sew Nose to end of Muzzle as in photograph.

**SOLE PATCHES** (make 2)

Using size D-3 (3mm) hook and C, ch 2.

**Round 1 (RS)** 5 sc in 2nd ch from hook, 1 slip st in first sc, turn. 5 sts.

**Round 2** Ch 1 (does NOT count as st), 2 sc in each sc to end, 1 slip st in first sc, turn. 10 sts.

**Round 3** Ch 1 (does NOT count as st), [1 sc in next sc, 2 sc in next sc] 5 times, 1 slip st in first sc. 15 sts.

Fasten off.

**TOE PATCHES** (make 6)

Work as given for Sole Patches to end of round 1.

Fasten off.

Using photograph as a guide, sew 3 Toe Patches and one Sole Patch to base of each foot.

**TAIL**

Using size D-3 (3mm) hook and A, ch 2.

**Round 1 (RS)** 4 sc in 2nd ch from hook, 1 slip st in first sc, turn. 4 sts.

**Round 2** Ch 1 (does NOT count as st), 2 sc in each sc to end, 1 slip st in first sc, turn. 8 sts.

**Round 3** Ch 1 (does NOT count as st), 2 sc in first sc, 1 sc in each of next 2 sc, 2 sc in each of next 2 sc, 1 sc in each of next 2 sc, 2 sc in last sc, 1 slip st in first sc, turn. 12 sts.

**Round 4** Ch 1 (does NOT count as st), 1 sc in each sc to end, 1 slip st in first sc, turn.

**Rounds 5 to 7** As round 4.

Fasten off.

Fold Tail flat, then sew Tail to back of Body.

Using photograph as a guide and scrap of brown yarn, embroider eyes and mouth onto face, and claws onto paws.

# storage pots

• • • • • • • • • •

Crochet is a great textile for containers, as it is firmer than knitting and also offers interesting, but easy-to-work textures. These pots in three sizes make useful containers to store all those nursery odds and ends, from cotton wool to little toys.

I chose to crochet these in strong, bright colors, ideal for a boy's room, but you can easily change the colors if you prefer a more pastel, girly look.

They are worked in the round in single crochet, in Rowan's *Denim* and *Handknit Cotton* yarns, and make a good project for someone who has mastered the basics of crochet.

## Sizes

Finished pots are approximately 4, 6 or 8in/10, 15 or 20cm wide at upper edge and 6, 8 or 10in/15, 20 or 25cm tall.

## Yarns

**LARGE POT**

3 x 50g/1¾oz balls of Rowan *Denim* in **MC** (Nashville 225) and 1 ball in **A** (Tennessee 231)

1 x 50g/1¾oz ball of Rowan *Handknit Cotton* in each of **B** (Seafarer 318) and **C** (Gooseberry 219)

**MEDIUM POT**

2 x 50g/1¾oz balls of Rowan *Denim* in **MC** (Nashville 225) and 1 x 50g/1¾oz ball in **A** (Tennessee 231)

1 x 50g/1¾oz ball of Rowan *Handknit Cotton* in each of **C** (Gooseberry 219) and **D** (Flame 254)

**SMALL POT**

1 x 50g/1¾oz ball of Rowan *Denim* in each of **MC** (Nashville 225) and **A** (Tennessee 231)

1 x 50g/1¾oz ball of Rowan *Handknit Cotton* in each of **B** (Seafarer 318) and **E** (Slick 313)

**Note:** 1 ball of each of **A**, **B**, **C**, **D**, and **E** is sufficient for all three pots.

## Hooks

Size G-6 (4mm) crochet hook

## Gauge

**Before washing:** 17 sts and 20 rows to 4in/10cm measured over sc using MC and size G-6 (4mm) hook *or size to obtain correct gauge.*

**Gauge note:** Denim will shrink and fade when washed for the first time. These storage pots are designed for display purposes only and will shrink if washed.

## Abbreviations

See page 117.

## large pot

Using size G-6 (4mm) hook and MC, ch 2.

**Round 1 (RS)** 6 sc in 2nd ch from hook, 1 slip st in first sc, turn. 6 sts.

**Round 2** Ch 1 (does NOT count as st), 2 sc in each sc to end, 1 slip st in first sc, turn. 12 sts.

**Round 3** Ch 1 (does NOT count as st), [1 sc in next sc, 2 sc in next sc] 6 times, 1 slip st in first sc, turn. 18 sts.

**Round 4** Ch 1 (does NOT count as st), [1 sc in each of next 2 sc, 2 sc in next sc] 6 times, 1 slip st in first sc, turn. 24 sts.

**Round 5** Ch 1 (does NOT count as st), [1 sc in each of next 3 sc, 2 sc in next sc] 6 times, 1 slip st in first sc, turn. 30 sts.

**Round 6** Ch 1 (does NOT count as st), [1 sc in each of next 4 sc, 2 sc in next sc] 6 times, 1 slip st in first sc, turn. 36 sts.

**Round 7** Ch 1 (does NOT count as st), [1 sc in each of next 5 sc, 2 sc in next sc] 6 times, 1 slip st in first sc, turn. 42 sts.

**Round 8** Ch 1 (does NOT count as st), [1 sc in each of next 6 sc, 2 sc in next sc] 6 times, 1 slip st in first sc, turn. 48 sts.

**Round 9** Ch 1 (does NOT count as st), [1 sc in each of next 7 sc, 2 sc in next sc] 6 times, 1 slip st in first sc, turn. 54 sts.

**Round 10** Ch 1 (does NOT count as st), [1 sc in each of next 8 sc, 2 sc in next sc] 6 times, 1 slip st in first sc, turn. 60 sts.

**Round 11** Ch 1 (does NOT count as st), [1 sc in each of next 9 sc, 2 sc in next sc] 6 times, 1 slip st in first sc, turn. 66 sts.

**Round 12** Ch 1 (does NOT count as st), [1 sc in each of next 10 sc, 2 sc in next sc] 6 times, 1 slip st in first sc, turn. 72 sts.

**Round 13** Ch 1 (does NOT count as st), [1 sc in each of next 11 sc, 2 sc in next sc] 6 times, 1 slip st in first sc, turn. 78 sts.

**Round 14** Ch 1 (does NOT count as st), [1 sc in each of next 12 sc, 2 sc in next sc] 6 times, 1 slip st in first sc, turn. 84 sts.

**Round 15** Ch 1 (does NOT count as st), [1 sc in each of next 13 sc, 2 sc in next sc] 6 times, 1 slip st in first sc, turn. 90 sts.

**Round 16** Ch 1 (does NOT count as st), 1 sc in each sc to end, 1 slip st in first sc, turn.

## SHAPE SIDES

**Round 1 (RS)** Ch 4 (counts as first tr), skip sc at base of 4 ch, *1 dc in next sc, 1 hdc in next sc, 1 sc in next sc, 1 hdc in next sc, 1 dc in next sc**, 1 tr in next sc, rep from * to end, ending last rep at **, 1 slip st in top of 4 ch at beg of round, turn.

**Round 2** Ch 1 (does NOT count as st), 1 sc in same place as slip st at end of previous round, *1 sc in each of next 2 sts, skip 1 sc, 1 sc in each of next 2 sts**, 3 sc in next tr, rep from * to end, ending last rep at **, 2 sc in same place as sc at beg of round, 1 slip st in first sc, turn. 15 patt reps.

**Round 3** Ch 1 (does NOT count as st), 1 sc in same place as slip st at end of previous round, *1 sc in each of next 2 sc, skip 2 sc, 1 sc in each of next 2 sc**, 3 sc in next sc, rep from * to end, ending last rep at **, 2 sc in same place as sc at beg of round, 1 slip st in first sc, turn.

**Rounds 4 to 13** As round 3.

**Round 14** Ch 1 (does NOT count as st), 2 sc in same place as slip st at end of previous round, *1 sc in each of next 2 sc, skip 2 sc, 1 sc in each of next 2 sc**, 5 sc in next sc, rep from * to end, ending last rep at **, 3 sc in same place as sc at beg of round, 1 slip st in first sc, turn.

**Round 15** Ch 1 (does NOT count as st), 1 sc in same place as slip st at end of previous round, *1 sc in each of next 3 sc, skip 2 sc, 1 sc in each of next 3 sc**, 3 sc in next sc, rep from * to end, ending last rep at **, 2 sc in same place as sc at beg of round, 1 slip st in first sc, turn.

**Rounds 16 to 23** As round 15.

Join in A.

**Rounds 24 and 25** Using A, as round 15.

**Round 26** Using MC, ch 1 (does NOT count as st), 2 sc in same place as slip st at end of previous round, *1 sc in each of next 3 sc, skip 2 sc, 1 sc in each of next 3 sc**, 5 sc in next sc, rep from * to end, ending last rep at **, 3 sc in same place as sc at beg of round, 1 slip st in first sc, turn.

**Round 27** Using MC, ch 1 (does NOT count as st), 1 sc in

same place as slip st at end of previous round, *1 sc in each of next 4 sc, skip 2 sc, 1 sc in each of next 4 sc**, 3 sc in next sc, rep from * to end, ending last rep at **, 2 sc in same place as sc at beg of round, 1 slip st in first sc, turn.

This round forms patt for remainder of Pot.

Using A, work 2 rounds.

Break off A.

Using MC, work 2 rounds.

Join in B.

Using B, work 2 rounds.

Break off B.

Using MC, work 2 rounds.

Break off MC and join in C.

Using C, work 2 rounds.

Fasten off.

## medium pot

Work as given for Large Pot to end of round 11. 66 sts.

**Next round (WS)** Ch 1 (does NOT count as st), 1 sc in each sc to end, 1 slip st in first sc, turn.

### SHAPE SIDES

Work rounds 1 to 3 as given for Large Pot, noting that there will be 11 patt reps after round 2.

**Rounds 4 to 11** As round 3.

**Round 12** Ch 1 (does NOT count as st), 2 sc in same place as slip st at end of previous round, *1 sc in each of next 2 sc, skip 2 sc, 1 sc in each of next 2 sc**, 5 sc in next sc, rep from * to end, ending last rep at **, 3 sc in same place as sc at beg of round, 1 slip st in first sc, turn.

**Round 13** Ch 1 (does NOT count as st), 1 sc in same place as slip st at end of previous round, *1 sc in each of next 3 sc, skip 2 sc, 1 sc in each of next 3 sc**, 3 sc in next sc, rep from * to end, ending last rep at **, 2 sc in same place as sc at beg of round, 1 slip st in first sc, turn.

**Rounds 14 to 17** As round 13.

Join in A.

**Rounds 18 and 19** Using A, as round 13.

**Rounds 20 and 21** Using MC, as round 13.

**Round 22** Using A, ch 1 (does NOT count as st), 2 sc in same place as slip st at end of previous round, *1 sc in each of next 3 sc, skip 2 sc, 1 sc in each of next 3 sc**, 5 sc in next sc, rep from * to end, ending last rep at **, 3 sc in same place as sc at beg of round, 1 slip st in first sc, turn.

**Round 23** Using A, ch 1 (does NOT count as st), 1 sc in same place as slip st at end of previous round, *1 sc in each of next 4 sc, skip 2 sc, 1 sc in each of next 4 sc**, 3 sc in next sc, rep from * to end, ending last rep at **, 2 sc in same place as sc at beg of round, 1 slip st in first sc, turn.

This round forms patt for remainder of Pot.

Break off A.

Using MC, work 2 rounds.

Join in C.

Using C, work 2 rounds.

Break off C.

Using MC, work 2 rounds.

Break off MC and join in D.

Using D, work 2 rounds.

Fasten off.


## small pot

Work as given for Large Pot to end of round 7. 42 sts.

**Next round (WS)** Ch 1 (does NOT count as st), 1 sc in each sc to end, 1 slip st in first sc, turn.

**SHAPE SIDES**

Work rounds 1 to 3 as given for Large Pot, noting that there will be 7 patt reps after round 2.

**Rounds 4 to 9** As round 3.

**Round 10** Ch 1 (does NOT count as st), 2 sc in same place as slip st at end of previous round, *1 sc in each of next 2 sc, skip 2 sc, 1 sc in each of next 2 sc**, 5 sc in next sc, rep from * to end, ending last rep at **, 3 sc in same place as sc at beg of round, 1 slip st in first sc, turn.

**Round 11** Ch 1 (does NOT count as st), 1 sc in same place as slip st at end of previous round, *1 sc in each of next 3 sc, skip 2 sc, 1 sc in each of next 3 sc**, 3 sc in next sc, rep from * to end, ending last rep at **, 2 sc in same place as sc at beg of round, 1 slip st in first sc, turn.

Join in A.

**Rounds 12 and 13** Using A, as round 11.

**Rounds 14 and 15** Using MC, as round 11.

**Rounds 16 and 17** Using A, as round 11.

Break off A.

**Round 18** Using MC, ch 1 (does NOT count as st), 2 sc in same place as slip st at end of previous round, *1 sc in each of next 3 sc, skip 2 sc, 1 sc in each of next 3 sc**, 5 sc in next sc, rep from * to end, ending last rep at **, 3 sc in same place as sc at beg of round, 1 slip st in first sc, turn.

**Round 19** Using MC, ch 1 (does NOT count as st), 1 sc in same place as slip st at end of previous round, *1 sc in each of next 4 sc, skip 2 sc, 1 sc in each of next 4 sc**, 3 sc in next sc, rep from * to end, ending last rep at **, 2 sc in same place as sc at beg of round, 1 slip st in first sc, turn.

This round forms patt for remainder of Pot.

Join in B.

Using B, work 2 rounds.

Break off B.

Using MC, work 2 rounds.

Break off MC and join in E.

Using E, work 2 rounds.

Fasten off.


**Finishing**

Do NOT wash. Press lightly on WS following instructions on yarn label.

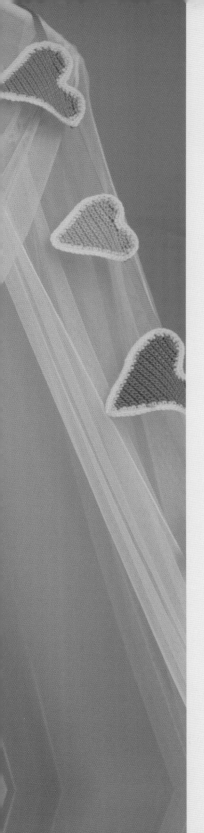

# string of hearts

• • • • • • • • • •

These heart motifs strung on a long ribbon make an ideal decoration for a baby crib or bed. Strung on a short ribbon, they look just as good hung along a shelf to decorate baby's room. They are really easy to make, and very portable.

In sugar-almond pastel colors, they are particularly pretty strung around a princess-style muslin bed or crib canopy.

Short strings of hearts can be embellished with bought satin roses or ribbons, for a pretty finishing touch, and would make a very sweet baby shower gift.

## Size

Short version is 5ft/1.5m long.

Completed string of hearts is 11yd/10m long.

## Yarns

### SHORT VERSION

1 x 50g/1¾oz ball of Rowan *RYC Cashsoft Baby DK* in each of **A** (Pixie 807 or Cloud 805) and **B** (Snowman 800)

### LONG VERSION

1 x 50g/1¾oz ball of Rowan *RYC Cashsoft Baby DK* in each of **A** (Pixie 807), **B** (Cloud 805), **C** (Crocus 808), **D** (Chicory 804), and **G** (Snowman 800)

1 x 50g/1¾oz ball of Rowan *RYC Cashsoft DK* in each of **E** (Sweet 501) and **F** (Glacier 504)

## Hook

Size G-6 (4mm) crochet hook

## Extras

³/₈in/1cm wide pink or blue ribbon—2¼yd/2m for short version or 11yd/10m for long version

5 ribbon roses for short version (optional)

Sewing thread for stitching ribbon to hearts

## Gauge

18 sts and 20 rows to 4in/10cm measured over sc using size G-6 (4mm) hook *or size to obtain correct gauge.*

## Abbreviations

See page 117.

## short version

**Large heart** (make 1)

Using size G-6 (4mm) hook and A, ch 2.

**Row 1 (RS)** 3 sc in 2nd ch from hook, turn. 3 sts.

**Row 2** Ch 1 (does NOT count as st), 1 sc in each sc to end, turn.

**Row 3** Ch 1 (does NOT count as st), 2 sc in first sc, 1 sc in next sc, 2 sc in last sc, turn. 5 sts.

**Row 4** Ch 1 (does NOT count as st), 1 sc in each sc to end, turn.

**Row 5** Ch 1 (does NOT count as st), 2 sc in first sc, 1 sc in each sc to last sc, 2 sc in last sc, turn. 7 sts.

**Rows 6 to 15** As rows 4 and 5, 5 times. 17 sts.

**Rows 16 to 19** As row 2.

### SHAPE TOP

**Row 20** Ch 1 (does NOT count as st), 1 sc in each of next 8 sc and turn, leaving rem sts unworked. 8 sts.

**Row 21** Ch 1 (does NOT count as st), 1 sc in each st to last 2 sts, sc2tog over last 2 sc, turn. 7 sts.

**Rows 22 and 23** As row 21. 5 sts.

**Row 24** Ch 1 (does NOT count as st), sc2tog over first 2 sts, 1 sc in next sc, sc2tog over last 2 sc. 3 sts. Fasten off.

Return to top of row 19, skip center sc, rejoin yarn to next sc and cont as foll:

**Row 20** Ch 1 (does NOT count as st), 1 sc in st where yarn was rejoined, 1 sc in each sc to end, turn. 8 sts.

**Row 21** Ch 1 (does NOT count as st), sc2tog over first 2 sc, 1 sc in each st to end, turn. 7 sts.

**Rows 22 and 23** As row 21. 5 sts.

**Row 24** Ch 1 (does NOT count as st), sc2tog over first 2 sts, 1 sc in next sc, sc2tog over last 2 sc. 3 sts. Fasten off.

### EDGING

With RS facing, using size G-6 (4mm) hook and B, attach yarn to base of heart, ch 1 (does NOT count as st), work in sc evenly around entire heart shape, working 3 sc in base of heart and ending with 1 slip st in first sc.

**Next round (RS)** Ch 1 (does NOT count as st), 1 sc in each sc to end, working 3 sc in base point and ending with 1 slip st in first sc. Fasten off.

**Medium heart** (make 2)

Work as given for large heart to end of row 5.

**Rows 6 to 11** As rows 4 and 5, 3 times. 13 sts.

**Rows 12 to 15** As row 2.

SHAPE TOP

**Row 16** Ch 1 (does NOT count as st), sc2tog over first 2 sc, 1 sc in each of next 4 sc and turn, leaving rem sts unworked. 5 sts.

**Row 17** Ch 1 (does NOT count as st), sc2tog over first 2 sc, 1 sc in each st to end, turn. 4 sts.

**Row 18** Ch 1 (does NOT count as st), sc2tog over first 2 sts, sc2tog over last 2 sc. 2 sts.

Fasten off.

Return to top of row 15, skip center sc, rejoin yarn to next sc and cont as foll:

**Row 16** Ch 1 (does NOT count as st), 1 sc in st where yarn was rejoined, 1 sc in each of next 4 sc, sc2tog over last 2 sc, turn. 5 sts.

**Row 17** Ch 1 (does NOT count as st), 1 sc in each of first 3 sts, sc2tog over last 2 sc, turn. 4 sts.

**Row 18** Ch 1 (does NOT count as st), sc2tog over first 2 sts, sc2tog over last 2 sc. 2 sts.

Fasten off.

EDGING

Work as given for large heart.

**Small heart** (make 2)

Work as given for large heart to end of row 5.

**Rows 6 and 7** As rows 4 and 5. 9 sts.

**Rows 8 to 10** As row 2.

SHAPE TOP

**Row 11** Ch 1 (does NOT count as st), 1 sc in each of first

4 sc and turn, leaving rem sts unworked. 4 sts.

**Row 12** Ch 1 (does NOT count as st), sc2tog over first 2 sts, sc2tog over last 2 sc. 2 sts.

Fasten off.

Return to top of row 10, skip center sc, rejoin yarn to next sc and cont as foll:

**Row 11** Ch 1 (does NOT count as st), 1 sc in st where yarn was rejoined, 1 sc in each of last 3 sc, turn. 4 sts.

**Row 12** Ch 1 (does NOT count as st), sc2tog over first 2 sts, sc2tog over last 2 sc. 2 sts.

Fasten off.

**EDGING**

Work as given for large heart.

### Finishing

Press lightly on WS following instructions on yarn label. Cut 26in/65cm length of ribbon and sew a ribbon bow to each end. Using photograph as a guide, sew ribbon to back of hearts. Sew a small bow to top of each heart, and add a ribbon rose to each bow if required.

## long version

### Large hearts

Using G for edging of all hearts, make 24 large hearts as for short version, making 4 each using A, B, C, D, E, and F.

### Medium hearts

Using G for edging of all hearts, make 24 medium hearts as for short version, making 4 each using A, B, C, D, E, and F.

### Finishing

Press lightly on WS following instructions on yarn label. Sew ribbon to back of Hearts.

*gallery of projects*

# stripy cat

• • • • • • • • • •

Bright colors grab the eye, and all small children are drawn to them. This little cat is no exception. With its rows of contrasting stripes, in lots of different colorways, and its touchingly large head, it has just the wow factor that all kids' toys require.

In machine-washable Rowan *Cotton Glacé* and *RYC Cashcotton*, with similarly washable toy filling, it will survive all the tough situations that its young handler is likely to put it through!

*gallery of projects*

### Size

Finished cat is approximately 8½in/22cm from nose to tip of tail.

### Yarns

1 x 50g/1¾oz ball of Rowan *Cotton Glacé* in each of **A** (Bleached 726), **B** (Pier 809), **C** (In The Pink 819), **D** (Poppy 814), **E** (Shoot 814), **F** (Maritime 817), and **G** (Black 727)
1 x 50g/1¾oz ball of Rowan *RYC Cashcotton 4 ply* in **H** (Imp 905)

### Hook

Size C-2 (2.5mm) crochet hook

### Extras

Washable toy filling
Scrap of black yarn (for face embroidery)

### Gauge

22 sts and 25 rows to 4in/10cm measured over sc using size C-2 (2.5mm) hook or *size to obtain correct gauge.*

### Abbreviations

See page 117.

### Left front leg

Using size C-2 (2.5mm) hook and D, ch 2.
**Round 1 (RS)** 9 sc in 2nd ch from hook, 1 slip st in first sc, turn. 9 sts.
**Round 2** Ch 1 (does NOT count as st), 2 sc in each sc to end, 1 slip st in first sc, turn. 18 sts.
**Round 3** Ch 1 (does NOT count as st), 1 sc in each sc to end, 1 slip st in first sc, turn.

*stripy cat*

Break off D and join in G.

**Rounds 4** As round 3.

Break off G and join in A.

**Rounds 5 and 6** As round 3.

Join in E.

**Round 7** Using E, ch 1 (does NOT count as st), 1 sc in each of first 7 sc, [sc2tog over next 2 sc] twice, 1 sc in each of last 7 sc, 1 slip st in first sc, turn. 16 sts.

**Round 8** Using E, as round 3.

**Round 9** Using A, ch 1 (does NOT count as st), sc2tog over first 2 sc, 1 sc in each of next 4 sc, [sc2tog over next 2 sc] twice, 1 sc in each of next 4 sc, sc2tog over last 2 sc, 1 slip st in first sc2tog, turn. 12 sts.

**Round 10** Using A, ch 1 (does NOT count as st), 1 sc in each of first 5 sc, sc2tog over next 2 sc, 1 sc in each of last 5 sc, 1 slip st in first sc, turn. 11 sts.

**Rounds 11 and 12** Using E, as round 3.

**Rounds 13 and 14** Using A, as round 3.

**Rounds 15 and 16** Using E, as round 3.

Fasten off.

Insert toy filling so that foot section is firmly filled and leg section is quite soft.

### Right front leg

Work as given for Left Front Leg, using C instead of D, F instead of A, and B instead of E.

### Left back leg

Using size C-2 (2.5mm) hook and C, ch 4.

**Round 1 (RS)** 2 sc in 2nd ch from hook, 1 sc in next ch, 6 sc in last ch, working back along foundation ch edge: 1 sc in next ch, 2 sc in same ch as first 2 sc, 1 slip st in first sc, turn. 12 sts.

**Round 2** Ch 1 (does NOT count as st), 2 sc in each sc to end, 1 slip st in first sc, turn. 24 sts.

**Round 3** Ch 1 (does NOT count as st), 1 sc in each sc to end,

1 slip st in first sc, turn.

Break off C and join in G.

**Round 4** As round 3.

Break off G and join in B.

**Rounds 5 and 6** As round 3.

Join in F.

**Round 7** Using F, ch 1 (does NOT count as st), 1 sc in each of first 10 sc, [sc2tog over next 2 sc] twice, 1 sc in each of last 10 sc, 1 slip st in first sc, turn. 22 sts.

**Round 8** Using F, ch 1 (does NOT count as st), 1 sc in each of first 9 sc, [sc2tog over next 2 sc] twice, 1 sc in each of last 9 sc, 1 slip st in first sc, turn. 20 sts.

**Round 9** Using B, ch 1 (does NOT count as st), sc2tog over first 2 sc, 1 sc in each of next 6 sc, [sc2tog over next 2 sc] twice, 1 sc in each of next 6 sc, sc2tog over last 2 sc, 1 slip st in first sc2tog, turn. 16 sts.

**Round 10** Using B, ch 1 (does NOT count as st), 1 sc in each of first 7 sc, sc2tog over next 2 sc, 1 sc in each of last 7 sc, 1 slip st in first sc, turn. 15 sts.

**Rounds 11 and 12** Using F, as round 3.

**Rounds 13 and 14** Using B, as round 3.

**Rounds 15 and 16** Using F, as round 3.

Fasten off.

Insert toy filling so that foot section is firmly filled and leg section is quite soft.

### Right back leg

Work as given for Left Back Leg, using D instead of C, E instead of B, and A instead of F.

### Tail

Using size C-2 (2.5mm) hook and G, ch 2.

**Round 1 (RS)** 4 sc in 2nd ch from hook, 1 slip st in first sc, turn. 4 sts.

**Round 2** Ch 1 (does NOT count as st), 2 sc in each sc to end, 1 slip st in first sc, turn. 8 sts.

**Round 3** Ch 1 (does NOT count as st), 1 sc in each sc to end, 1 slip st in first sc, turn.
Break off G and join in B.
**Rounds 4 to 15** As round 3.
Now work in rows as foll:
**Row 16** Ch 1 (does NOT count as st), sc2tog over first 2 sc, 1 sc in each of next 4 sc, sc2tog over last 2 sc, turn. 6 sts.
**Row 17** Ch 1 (does NOT count as st), sc2tog over first 2 sts, 1 sc in each of next 2 sc, sc2tog over last 2 sts, turn. 4 sts.
**Row 18** Ch 1 (does NOT count as st), sc2tog over first 2 sts, sc2tog over last 2 sts. 2 sts.
Fasten off.

**Underbody**
Using size C-2 (2.5mm) hook and H, ch 9.
**Row 1 (RS)** 1 sc in 2nd ch from hook, 1 sc in each ch to end, turn. 8 sts.
**Row 2** Ch 1 (does NOT count as st), 2 sc in first sc, 1 sc in each sc to last sc, 2 sc in last sc, turn. 10 sts.
**Rows 3 and 4** As row 2. 14 sts.
**Row 5** Ch 1 (does NOT count as st), 1 sc in each sc to end, turn.
**Row 6** As row 2. 16 sts.
**Rows 7 to 14** As row 5.
**Row 15** Ch 1 (does NOT count as st), sc2tog over first 2 sts, 1 sc in each sc to last 2 sts, sc2tog over last 2 sts, turn. 14 sts.
**Rows 16 and 17** As row 5.
**Row 18** As row 15. 12 sts.
**Row 19** As row 5.
**Rows 20 to 22** As row 15. 6 sts. Fasten off.

**Upperbody**
Using size C-2 (2.5mm) hook and C, ch 7.
**Row 1 (RS)** 1 sc in 2nd ch from hook, 1 sc in each of next

4 ch, 4 sc in last ch, working back along other side of foundation ch 1 sc in each of next 5 ch, turn. 14 sts.
**Row 2** Ch 1 (does NOT count as st), 1 sc in each of first 6 sc, 2 sc in each of next 2 sc, 1 sc in each of last 6 sc, turn. 16 sts.
**Row 3** Ch 1 (does NOT count as st), 1 sc in each of first 7 sc, 2 sc in each of next 2 sc, 1 sc in each of last 7 sc, turn. 18 sts.
**Row 4** Ch 1 (does NOT count as st), 1 sc in each of first 8 sc, 2 sc in each of next 2 sc, 1 sc in each of last 8 sc, turn. 20 sts.
**Row 5** Ch 1 (does NOT count as st), 1 sc in each sc to end, turn.
**Row 6** Ch 1 (does NOT count as st), 1 sc in each of first 9 sc, 2 sc in each of next 2 sc, 1 sc in each of last 9 sc, turn. 22 sts.
**Rows 7 to 16** As row 5.
**Row 17** Ch 1 (does NOT count as st), 1 sc in each of first 9 sc, [sc2tog over next 2 sc] twice, 1 sc in each of last 9 sc, turn. 20 sts.
**Rows 18 and 19** As row 5.
**Row 20** Ch 1 (does NOT count as st), 1 sc in each of first 8 sc, [sc2tog over next 2 sc] twice, 1 sc in each of last 8 sc, turn. 18 sts.
**Row 21** As row 5.
**Row 22** Ch 1 (does NOT count as st), 1 sc in each of first 7 sc, [sc2tog over next 2 sc] twice, 1 sc in each of last 7 sc, turn. 16 sts.
**Row 23** As row 5.
**Row 24** Ch 1 (does NOT count as st), 1 sc in each of first 6 sc, [sc2tog over next 2 sc] twice, 1 sc in each of last 6 sc, turn. 14 sts.
**Row 25** Ch 1 (does NOT count as st), 1 sc in each of first 5 sc, [sc2tog over next 2 sc] twice, 1 sc in each of last 5 sc, turn. 12 sts.
**Row 26** Ch 1 (does NOT count as st), 1 sc in each of first

4 sc, [sc2tog over next 2 sc] twice, 1 sc in each of last 4 sc, turn. 10 sts.

**Row 27** Ch 1 (does NOT count as st), 1 sc in each of first 3 sc, [sc2tog over next 2 sc] twice, 1 sc in each of last 3 sc, turn. 8 sts.

Fold Upperbody in half with RS together and join front seam by working in sc across top of last row, working each st through both layers.

Fasten off.

### Head

Using size C-2 (2.5mm) hook and D, ch 2.

**Round 1 (RS)** 8 sc in 2nd ch from hook, 1 slip st in first sc, turn. 8 sts.

**Round 2** Ch 1 (does NOT count as st), 2 sc in each sc to end, 1 slip st in first sc, turn. 16 sts.

**Round 3** Ch 1 (does NOT count as st), [2 sc in next sc, 1 sc in next sc] 8 times, 1 slip st in first sc, turn. 24 sts.

**Round 4** Ch 1 (does NOT count as st), 1 sc in each sc to end, 1 slip st in first sc, turn.

**Round 5** Ch 1 (does NOT count as st), [2 sc in next sc, 1 sc in each of next 2 sc] 8 times, 1 slip st in first sc, turn. 32 sts.

**Round 6** As round 4.

**Round 7** Ch 1 (does NOT count as st), [2 sc in next sc, 1 sc in each of next 3 sc] 8 times, 1 slip st in first sc, turn. 40 sts.

**Rounds 8 to 15** As round 4.

**Round 16** Ch 1 (does NOT count as st), [1 sc in each of next 3 sc, sc2tog over next 2 sc] 8 times, 1 slip st in first sc, turn. 32 sts.

**Round 17** As round 4.

**Round 18** Ch 1 (does NOT count as st), [1 sc in each of next 2 sc, sc2tog over next 2 sc] 8 times, 1 slip st in first sc, turn. 24 sts.

Insert toy filling in Head.

Inserting a little more toy filling as required, cont as foll:

Break off D and join in A.

**Rounds 19 and 20** As round 4.

**Round 21** Ch 1 (does NOT count as st), [1 sc in next sc, sc2tog over next 2 sc] 8 times, 1 slip st in first sc, turn. 16 sts.

**Rounds 22 and 23** As round 4.

**Round 24** Ch 1 (does NOT count as st), [sc2tog over next 2 sc] 8 times, 1 slip st in first sc, turn. 8 sts.

**Round 25** Ch 1 (does NOT count as st), [sc2tog over next 2 sc] 4 times, 1 slip st in first sc. 4 sts.

Fasten off.

### Ears (make 2)

Using size C-2 (2.5mm) hook and H, ch 2.

**Row 1 (RS)** 3 sc in 2nd ch from hook, turn. 3 sts.

**Row 2** Ch 1 (does NOT count as st), 1 sc in first sc, 3 sc in next sc, 1 sc in last sc, turn. 5 sts.

**Row 3** Ch 1 (does NOT count as st), 1 sc in each of first 2 sc, 3 sc in next sc, 1 sc in each of last 2 sc, turn. 7 sts.

**Row 4** Ch 1 (does NOT count as st), 1 sc in each of first 3 sc, 3 sc in next sc, 1 sc in each of last 3 sc, turn. 9 sts.

**Row 5** Ch 1 (does NOT count as st), 1 sc in each of first 4 sc, 3 sc in next sc, 1 sc in each of last 4 sc, turn. 11 sts.

Break off H and join in E.

**Rows 6 and 7** Ch 1 (does NOT count as st), 1 sc in each sc to end, turn.

**Row 8** Ch 1 (does NOT count as st), 1 sc in each of first 3 sc, sc2tog over next 2 sc, 1 sc in next sc, sc2tog over next 2 sc, 1 sc in each of last 3 sc, turn. 9 sts.

**Row 9** Ch 1 (does NOT count as st), 1 sc in each of first 2 sc, sc2tog over next 2 sc, 1 sc in next sc, sc2tog over next 2 sc, 1 sc in each of last 2 sc, turn. 7 sts.

**Row 10** Ch 1 (does NOT count as st), 1 sc in first sc, [sc2tog over next 2 sc, 1 sc in next sc] twice, turn. 5 sts.

**Row 11** Ch 1 (does NOT count as st), sc2tog over first 2 sc, 1 sc in next sc, sc2tog over last 2 sc, turn. 3 sts.

Fasten off.

## Finishing

Do NOT press.

Sew Underbody to Upperbody, matching center of foundation ch edge of Underbody to end of first row of Upperbody and center of last row of Underbody to beg of last row of Upperbody, and leaving a small opening. Turn body right side out, insert toy filling, and sew opening closed.

Fold top of Legs flat, with fasten-off point at one folded edge, and sew Legs to body seam, positioning Legs as in photograph.

Fold top of Tail flat, with fasten-off point at one folded edge, and sew Tail to end of body as in photograph.

Using photograph as a guide, sew Head to body. Fold ears flat, then sew to sides of Head as in photograph.

Using photograph as a guide and scrap of black yarn, embroider eyes onto head.

Using C, embroider nose in satin stitch over center of face as shown, and mouth in backstitch below nose.

*stripy cat*

# bibs

● ● ● ● ● ● ● ● ● ●

Made simply in single crochet and chain stitches, these bibs can be made in no time at all, so even if you have never crocheted before, you will be able to make them easily. There are three different versions—a simple stripy one and two others with appliqué motifs. They come in two colorways—shades of pink and white for girls, and shades of blue and white for boys.

Make a little set of three to give as a gift for a new baby, with a neat little crochet card (see page 109) and a crochet gift ribbon (see page 110).

## Sizes
Finished bib is approximately 6¼in/16cm wide.

## Yarns
1 x 50g/1¾oz ball of Rowan *4 ply Cotton* in each of **A** (Bleached 113), **B** (Orchid 120 or Opaque 112), **C** (Cheeky 133 or Cooking Apple 137), and **D** (Bloom 132 or Aegean 129)

## Hooks
Size E-4 (3.5mm) crochet hook

## Gauge
First 5 rounds measure 2⅛in/5.5cm in diameter using size E-4 (3.5mm) hook *or size to obtain correct gauge.*

## Abbreviations
See page 117.

## bib with two motifs

Using size E-4 (3.5mm) hook and A, ch 5 and join with a slip st to first ch to form a ring.

**Round 1 (RS)** Ch 1 (does NOT count as st), 12 sc in ring, 1 slip st in first sc. 12 sts.

**Round 2** Ch 1 (does NOT count as st), working in back loops only of sts of previous round: *1 sc in next sc, ch 1, rep from * to end, 1 slip st in first sc. 24 sts.

**Round 3** Ch 1 (does NOT count as st), working in back loops only of sts of previous round: *[1 sc in next st, ch 1] twice, skip 1 st, 1 sc in next st, ch 1, rep from * to end, 1 slip st in first sc. 36 sts.

**Round 4** Ch 1 (does NOT count as st), working in back loops only of previous round: *1 sc in next sc, ch 1, skip 1 ch, rep from * to end, 1 slip st in first sc.

**Rounds 5 and 6** As rounds 3 and 4. 54 sts.

**Round 7** Ch 1 (does NOT count as st), working into back loops only of sts of previous round: *1 sc in next st, ch 1, skip 1 st, 1 sc in next st, ch 1, rep from * to end, 1 slip st in first sc. 72 sts.

**Round 8** As round 4 but turn at end of round.

Now working in rows, not rounds, shape neck edge as foll:

**Row 9 (WS)** Ch 1 (does NOT count as st), working into front loops only of sts of previous round: [1 sc in next st, ch 1, skip 1 st, 1 sc in next st, ch 1] 20 times, 1 sc in next st, ch 1, skip 1 st, 1 sc in next st and turn, leaving rem 9 sts unworked. 83 sts.

**Row 10** Ch 1 (does NOT count as st), working into back loops only of sts of previous row: skip first 2 sts, [1 sc in next sc, ch 1, skip 1 ch] 39 times, 1 sc in next st and turn, leaving rem 2 sts unworked. 79 sts.

**Row 11** Ch 1 (does NOT count as st), working into front loops only of sts of previous row: skip first 2 sts, *[1 sc in next st, ch 1, skip 1 st] twice, 1 sc in next st, ch 1, rep from * 13 times more, [1 sc in next st, ch 1, skip 1 st] twice, 1 sc in next st and turn, leaving rem 2 sts unworked. 89 sts.

**Row 12** Ch 1 (does NOT count as st), working into back loops only of sts of previous row: skip first 2 sts, [1 sc in next sc, ch 1, skip 1 ch] 42 times, 1 sc in next st and turn, leaving rem 2 sts unworked. 85 sts.

**Row 13** Ch 1 (does NOT count as st), working into front loops only of sts of previous row: *[1 sc in next st, ch 1, skip 1 st] twice, 1 sc in next st, ch 1, rep from * 15 times more, [1 sc in next st, ch 1, skip 1 st] twice, 1 sc in last sc, turn. 101 sts.

Break off A and join in C.

**Row 14** Using C, ch 1 (does NOT count as st), working into back loops only of sts of previous row: 1 sc in first sc, *ch 1, skip 1 ch, 1 sc in next sc, rep from * to end, turn.

Join in B.

**Row 15** Using B, ch 1 (does NOT count as st), working into front loops only of sts of previous row: 1 sc in first sc, *ch 1, skip 1 ch, 1 sc in next sc, rep from * to end, turn.
Break off B.
**Row 16** As row 14.
Fasten off.

## bib with one motif

Work as given for Bib with Two Motifs using colors as foll:
**Rounds 1 to 8** Using B.
**Rows 9 to 12** Using B.

**Row 13** Using C.
**Rows 14 and 15** Using A.
**Row 16** Using C.

## striped bib

Work as given for Bib with Two Motifs using colors as foll:
**Round 1** Using A.
**Round 2** Using B.
**Round 3** Using C.
**Round 4** Using D.
Rep these 4 rounds (or rows) 3 times more.

### Finishing

Press lightly on WS following instructions on yarn label.

**NECK TIE**

Using size E-4 (3.5mm) hook and A, ch 50, with RS facing, work 23 sc evenly around neck slope, ch 51 and turn.

**Row 1 (WS)** 1 sc in 2nd ch from hook, 1 sc in each of next 49 ch, 1 sc in each of next 23 sc, 1 sc in each of last 50 ch.

Fasten off.

**GIRL'S VERSIONS**

**MOTIF FOR BIB WITH ONE MOTIF**

Using size E-4 (3.5mm) hook and A, ch 8 and join with a slip st to first ch to form a ring.

**Round 1** Ch 1 (does NOT count as st), 16 sc in ring, 1 slip st in first sc. 16 sts.

**Row 2** Ch 11 (counts as first dc and 8 ch), skip sc at base of 11 ch and next sc, [1 dc in next sc, ch 8, skip 1 sc] 5 times, 1 dc in next sc, turn.

**Row 3** [1 sc, 1 hdc, 1 dc, 3 tr, ch 4, 1 slip st in top of last tr, 2 tr, 1 dc, 1 hdc and 1 sc] in each ch sp to end, 1 slip st in 3rd of 11 ch at beg of previous row.

Fasten off.

**MOTIF FOR BIB WITH TWO MOTIFS** (make 2)

Using size E-4 (3.5mm) hook and B, ch 6 and join with a slip st to first ch to form a ring.

**Row 1** Ch 1 (does NOT count as st), 7 sc in ring, turn. 17 sts.

**Row 2** Ch 11 (counts as first dc and 8 ch), skip sc at base of 11 ch and next sc, [1 dc in next sc, ch 8, skip 1 sc] twice, 1 dc in last sc, turn.

**Row 3** [1 sc, 1 hdc, 1 dc, 3 tr, ch 4, 1 slip st in top of last tr, 2 tr, 1 dc, 1 hdc and 1 sc] in each ch sp to end, 1 slip st in 3rd of 11 ch at beg of previous row.

Fasten off.

Using photograph as a guide, sew Motifs to Bibs. Using C, embroider French knots as in photograph.

**BOY'S VERSIONS**

**MOTIF FOR BIB WITH ONE MOTIF**

Using size E-4 (3.5mm) hook and A, ch 5 and join with a slip st to first ch to form a ring.

**Round 1** Ch 7 (counts as first tr and 3 ch), [1 tr in ring, ch 3] 8 times, 1 slip st in 4th of 7 ch at beg of round.

**Round 2** Ch 3 (counts as first dc), [4 dc in next ch sp, 1 dc in next tr] 8 times, 4 dc in next ch sp, 1 slip st in top of 3 ch at beg of round.

**Row 3** Ch 1 (does NOT count as st), 1 sc in first dc, [ch 6, 1 sc in 2nd ch from hook, 1 hdc in next ch, 1 dc in next ch, 1 tr in next ch, 1 dtr in next ch, skip 4 dc of round 2, 1 sc in next dc] 8 times.

Fasten off.

**MOTIF FOR BIB WITH TWO MOTIFS** (make 2)

Using size E-4 (3.5mm) hook and B, ch 5 and join with a slip st to first ch to form a ring.

**Row 1** Ch 7 (counts as first tr and 3 ch), [1 tr in ring, ch 3] 3 times, 1 tr in ring, turn.

**Row 2** Ch 3 (counts as first dc), [4 dc in next ch sp, 1 dc in next tr] 4 times, working dc at end of last rep in 4th of 7 ch at beg of previous row.

**Row 3** Ch 1 (does NOT count as st), 1 sc in first dc, [ch 6, 1 sc in 2nd ch from hook, 1 hdc in next ch, 1 dc in next ch, 1 tr in next ch, 1 dtr in next ch, skip 4 dc of round 2, 1 sc in next dc] 4 times.

Fasten off.

Using photograph as a guide, sew Motifs to Bibs. Using D, embroider French knots as in photograph.

# wrap cardigan

• • • • • • • • •

This simple wrap cardigan is wonderfully easy to crochet and just as easy for baby to wear. It is pretty enough to wear as a cover-up over a party dress, too.

The simple crossover design with ties means that fit is not an issue, and it is crocheted in light and airy doubles, in delightfully soft Rowan *RYC Cashsoft Baby 4 ply*.

Someone who has mastered the basics of crochet and wants to try their skills on some simple shaping will love this project.

**To fit age, approximately**

| 0–3 | 3–6 | 6–12 | 12–18 | months |
|---|---|---|---|---|
| **Chest** | | | | |
| 16 | 18 | 20 | 22 | in |
| 41 | 46 | 51 | 56 | cm |

**Finished measurements**

**AROUND CHEST**

| 17¼ | 20½ | 21½ | 24 | in |
|---|---|---|---|---|
| 44 | 51 | 55 | 61 | cm |

**LENGTH FROM SHOULDER**

| 6¼ | 7¾ | 9 | 11 | in |
|---|---|---|---|---|
| 16 | 20 | 23 | 28 | cm |

**SLEEVE SEAM**

| 4¾ | 6 | 7½ | 9 | in |
|---|---|---|---|---|
| 12 | 15 | 19 | 23 | cm |

### Yarns

2 (3: 3: 4) x 50g/1¾oz balls of Rowan *RYC Cashsoft Baby 4 ply* in Spa 424

### Hook

Size D-3 (3mm) crochet hook

### Extras

2 snaps

### Gauge

21 sts and 12 rows to 4in/10cm measured over patt using size D-3 (3mm) hook *or size to obtain correct gauge.*

### Abbreviations

**dc2tog** = [yo and insert hook in next st, yo and draw loop through, yo and draw through 2 loops] twice, yo and draw through all 3 loops on hook; **dc3tog** = [yo and insert hook in next st, yo and draw loop through, yo and draw through 2 loops] 3 times, yo and draw through all

4 loops on hook.
See also page 117.

### Shaping note

All decreases are worked as foll:

**To dec 1 st at beg of row:** ch 3 (counts as first dc), skip dc at base of 3 ch, dc2tog over next 2 sts, patt to end.

**To dec 1 st at end of row:** patt to last 3 sts, dc2tog over next 2 sts, 1 dc in top of turning ch at beg of previous row, turn.

**To dec 2 sts at beg of row:** ch 3 (counts as first dc), skip dc at base of 3 ch, dc3tog over next 3 sts, patt to end.

**To dec 2 sts at end of row:** patt to last 4 sts, dc3tog over next 3 sts, 1 dc in top of turning ch at beg of previous row, turn.

All increases are worked as foll:

**To inc 1 st at beg of row:** ch 3 (counts as first dc), skip dc at base of 3 ch, 2 dc in next dc, patt to end.

**To inc 1 st at end of row:** patt to last 2 sts, 2 dc in next dc, 1 dc in top of turning ch at beg of previous row, turn.

### Body (worked in one piece to armholes)

Using size D-3 (3mm) hook, ch 126 (142: 158: 174).

**Foundation row (RS)** 1 dc in 4th ch from hook, 1 dc in each ch to end, turn. 124 (140: 156: 172) sts.

**Next row** Ch 3 (counts as first dc), skip dc at base of 3 ch, 1 dc in each dc to end, working last dc in top of 3 ch at beg of previous row, turn.

Last row forms dc fabric.

### SHAPE FRONT SLOPES

Cont in dc, dec 2 sts at each end of next 5 (9: 8: 6) rows, then 0 (0: 1: 1) st at each end of foll 0 (0: 3: 9) rows, ending with WS facing for next row. 104 (104: 118: 130) sts.

### SHAPE LEFT FRONT

**Next row (WS)** Ch 3 (counts as first dc), [dc3tog over next 3 sts] 1 (0: 0: 0) time, [dc2tog over next 2 sts] 0 (1: 1: 1) time, 1 dc in each of next 22 (20: 24: 27) dc and turn, leaving rem sts unworked.

Work on these 24 (22: 26: 29) sts only for left front.

Dec 2 sts at front slope edge of next 4 (0: 0: 0) rows, then 1 st at front slope edge of next 4 (7: 9: 10) rows then on foll 1 (2: 2: 2) alt rows **and at the same time** dec 1 st at armhole edge of next 3 (4: 5: 6) rows. 8 (9: 10: 11) sts.

Work 1 row.

### SHAPE SHOULDER

Fasten off.

### SHAPE BACK

Return to last complete row worked, skip next 6 dc, rejoin yarn to next dc and cont as foll:

**Next row (WS)** Ch 3 (counts as first dc), skip dc at base of 3 ch (this is dc where yarn was rejoined), 1 dc in each of

next 39 (45: 51: 57) dc and turn, leaving rem sts unworked.

Work on these 40 (46: 52: 58) sts only for back.

Dec 1 st at each end of next 3 (4: 5: 6) rows. 34 (38: 42: 46) sts.

Work 6 (6: 7: 7) rows.

### SHAPE BACK NECK

**Next row** Ch 3 (counts as first dc), skip dc at base of 3 ch, 1 dc in each of next 8 (9: 10: 11) dc and turn, leaving rem sts unworked.

Dec 1 st at neck edge of next row. 8 (9: 10: 11) sts.

### SHAPE SHOULDER

Fasten off.

Return to last complete row worked before shaping back neck, skip next 16 (18: 20: 22) dc, rejoin yarn to next dc and

cont as foll:

**Next row (WS)** Ch 3 (counts as first dc), skip dc at base of 3 ch (this is dc where yarn was rejoined), 1 dc in each of next 8 (9: 10: 11) sts, turn.

Dec 1 st at neck edge of next row. 8 (9: 10: 11) sts.

### SHAPE SHOULDER
Fasten off.

### SHAPE RIGHT FRONT

Return to last complete row worked before dividing for left front and back, skip next 6 dc, rejoin yarn to next dc and cont as foll:

**Next row (WS)** Ch 3 (counts as first dc), skip dc at base of 3 ch (this is dc where yarn was rejoined), 1 dc in each dc to last 4 (3: 3: 3) sts, [dc3tog over next 3 sts] 1 (0: 0: 0) time, [dc2tog over next 2 sts] 0 (1: 1: 1) time, 1 dc in top of 3 ch at beg of previous row, turn. 24 (22: 26: 29) sts.

Dec 2 sts at front slope edge of next 4 (0: 0: 0) rows, then 1 st at front slope edge of next 4 (7: 9: 10) rows then on foll 1 (2: 2: 2) alt rows and at same time dec 1 st at armhole edge of next 3 (4: 5: 6) rows. 8 (9: 10: 11) sts.

Work 1 row.

### SHAPE SHOULDER
Fasten off.

## Sleeves

Using size D-3 (3mm) hook, ch 30 (32: 34: 36).

Work foundation row as given for Body. 28 (30: 32: 34) sts.

Cont in dc fabric as given for Body, inc 1 st at each end of next 3 (1: 1: 1) rows, then on foll 4 (7: 9: 8) alt rows, then on 0 (0: 0: 2) foll 3rd rows. 42 (46: 52: 56) sts.

Work 1 (1: 2: 2) rows.

### SHAPE TOP

**Next row** Slip st across and in 4th st, ch 3 (counts as first dc), skip dc at base of 3 ch, 1 dc in each dc to last 3 sts and turn, leaving rem 3 sts unworked. 36 (40: 46: 50) sts.

Dec 2 sts at each end of next 5 (6: 7: 8) rows. 16 (16: 18:

18) sts. Fasten off.

## Finishing

Press lightly on WS following instructions on yarn label.

Sew shoulder seams.

### FRONT AND NECK EDGING

With RS facing and using size D-3 (3mm) hook, attach yarn to right front at foundation ch edge, ch 1 (does NOT count as st), work 1 row of sc evenly up right front slope, around back neck, and down left front slope to foundation ch edge, ensuring number of sc worked is divisible by 5 plus 1, turn.

**Next row (WS)** Ch 1 (does NOT count as st), 1 sc in each of first 3 sc, *ch 3, 1 slip st in top of last sc**, 1 sc in each of next 5 sc, rep from * to end, ending last rep at **, 1 sc in each of last 3 sc.

Fasten off.

### CUFF EDGINGS (both alike)

Work across foundation ch edge of Sleeve as given for Front and Neck Edging.

Sew sleeve seams. Matching top of sleeve seam to center of skipped sts at underarm and center of last row of Sleeve to shoulder seam, sew Sleeves into armholes.

Lay one front over other front (left over right for a boy, or right over left for a girl) and attach snaps to fasten row-end edges of fronts in place.

### BOW

Using size D-3 (3mm) hook, ch 52.

**Next row (WS)** 1 sc in 2nd ch from hook, 1 sc in each of next 2 ch, *ch 3, 1 slip st in top of last sc**, 1 sc in each of next 5 ch, rep from * to end, ending last rep at **, 1 sc in each of last 3 ch.

Fasten off.

Tie Bow into a bow and attach to front as in photograph.

# coat hangers

· · · · · · · · · ·

These decorative little crocheted coat hangers with their appliqué crochet motifs—a flower for a girl, a car for a boy—will cheer up any child's room and are great for hanging delicate knitted items that might otherwise slip off an ordinary hanger or be stretched out of shape by it.

They make a nice baby gift, too, and are very easy to work—great for a newcomer to crochet—so get in the groove and make a pair to give as presents.

## Size

Coat-hanger cover fits a child's wooden coat hanger approximately 12¼in/31cm wide.

## Yarns

**GIRL'S SET**

1 x 50g/1¾oz ball of Rowan *RYC Cashsoft Baby DK* in each of **A** (Pixie 807), **B** (Imp 803), and **D** (Chicory 804)

1 x 50g/1¾oz ball of Rowan *RYC Cashsoft DK* in **F** (Sweet 501)

1 x 50g/1¾oz ball of Rowan *RYC Cashsoft 4 ply* in each of **C** (Rose Lake 421) and **E** (Mosaic 426)

**BOY'S SET**

1 x 50g/1¾oz ball of Rowan *RYC Cashsoft Baby DK* in each of **A** (Cloud 805) and **E** (Savannah 507)

1 x 50g/1¾oz ball of Rowan *RYC Cashsoft DK* in each of **B** (Lime 509), **C** (Cream 500), and **D** (Donkey 517)

## Hook

Size E-4 (3.5mm) crochet hook
Size G-6 (4mm) crochet hook

## Extras

Piece of polyester batting
**Girl's set:** 16 beads; 30in/76cm of ribbon

## Gauge

18 sts and 20 rows to 4in/10cm measured over sc using size G-6 (4mm) hook *or size to obtain correct gauge.*

## Abbreviations

See page 117.

coat hangers

## girl's set (two colorways)

**Coat-hanger cover** (make 2 for each coat hanger)
Using size G-6 (4mm) hook and A, ch 2.
**Round 1 (RS)** 6 sc in 2nd ch from hook, 1 slip st in first sc, turn. 6 sts.
**Round 2** Ch 1 (does NOT count as st), 2 sc in each sc to end, 1 slip st in first sc, turn. 12 sts.
**Round 3** Ch 1 (does NOT count as st), 1 sc in each sc to end, 1 slip st in first sc, turn.
**Round 4** Ch 1 (does NOT count as st), [1 sc in next sc, 2 sc in next sc] 6 times, 1 slip st in first sc, turn. 18 sts.
**Round 5** As round 3.
**Round 6** Ch 1 (does NOT count as st), [1 sc in each of next 2 sc, 2 sc in next sc] 6 times, 1 slip st in first sc, turn. 24 sts.
**Rounds 7 to 36** As round 3.
Now working in rows, not rounds, complete cover as foll:
**Row 37** Slip st across and in 4th sc, ch 1 (does NOT count as st), 1 sc in sc at base of ch 1, 1 sc in each of next 17 sc and turn, leaving rem 3 sc unworked. 18 sts.
**Row 38** Slip st across and in 4th sc, ch 1 (does NOT count as st), 1 sc in sc at base of 1 ch, 1 sc in each of next 11 sc and turn, leaving rem 3 sc unworked. 12 sts.
**Row 39** Slip st across and in 4th sc, ch 1 (does NOT count as st), 1 sc in sc at base of 1 ch, 1 sc in each of next 5 sc.
Fasten off.
Make a second piece in exactly the same way.
For second coat-hanger cover, make another 2 pieces using D.

**Flower** (make 2)
Using size E-4 (3.5mm) hook and B, ch 7 and join with a slip st to first ch to form a ring.
**Round 1 (RS)** Ch 1 (does NOT count as st), 16 sc in ring, 1 slip st in first sc. 16 sts.
**Round 2** Ch 1 (does NOT count as st), 1 sc in first sc, [ch 5, skip 1 sc, 1 sc in next sc] 7 times, ch 5, skip 1 sc, 1 slip st in

first sc. Fasten off.
Join in C to one ch sp and cont as foll:
**Round 3** Ch 1 (does NOT count as st), [1 sc, 5 hdc and 1 sc] in each ch sp to end, 1 slip st in first sc.
Fasten off.

Make another flower in exactly the same way, but using E instead of B, and F instead of C.

## Finishing

Do NOT press.

Cut batting into 2in/5cm wide strips and carefully wrap batting around coat hanger to pad it out to approximately 1¼–1½in/3–4cm thick, securing batting with a few stitches. Slip crochet pieces over padded coat hanger so that tops of last row meet at center hook. Ensure batting is smooth and even inside cover, then sew two halves of cover together neatly where they meet at center.

Using photograph as a guide, sew on flowers just below hook. Sew beads around center of Flower as in photograph. Cut ribbon into two equal lengths and tie in a bow around base of hook.

## boy's set (two colorways)

**Coat-hanger cover** (make 2 for each coat hanger)
Work as for girl's set, making 2 pieces using A and 2 pieces using E.

**Car** (make 2)
Using size E-4 (3.5mm) hook and B, ch 19.
**Row 1 (RS)** 1 sc in 2nd ch from hook, 1 sc in each ch to end, turn. 18 sts.
**Row 2** Ch 1 (does NOT count as st), 1 sc in each sc to end, turn.
**Row 3** As row 2.
**Row 4** Ch 1 (does NOT count as st), 1 sc in each sc to last 2 sc, sc2tog over last 2 sc, turn. 17 sts.
**Row 5** Ch 1 (does NOT count as st), sc2tog over first 2 sts, 1 sc in each sc to last 2 sts, sc2tog over last 2 sts, turn. 15 sts.
**Row 6** As row 5. 13 sts.

Join in C.
**Row 7** Using B slip st across and in 3rd st, ch 1 (does NOT count as st), 1 sc in sc at base of 1 ch, 1 sc in next sc, using C 1 sc in each of next 2 sc, using B 1 sc in next sc, using C 1 sc in each of next 2 sc, using B 1 sc in each of next 2 sc and turn, leaving rem 2 sts unworked. 9 sts.
**Row 8** Using B ch 1 (does NOT count as st), 1 sc in each of first 2 sc, using C 1 sc in each of next 2 sc, using B 1 sc in next sc, using C 1 sc in each of next 2 sc, using B 1 sc in each of last 2 sc, turn.
Break off C.
**Row 9** As row 2.
**Rows 10 and 11** As row 5. 5 sts.
Fasten off.
Make another car in exactly the same way, but using A instead of B.

**Wheels** (make 2 for each car)
Using size E-4 (3.5mm) hook and C, ch 2.
**Round 1 (RS)** 5 sc in 2nd ch from hook, 1 slip st in first sc. 5 sts.
Break off C and join in D.
**Round 2** Ch 1 (does NOT count as st), 2 sc in each sc to end, 1 slip st in first sc.
Fasten off.
Make another 3 wheels in exactly the same way.

## Finishing

Do NOT press.
Make up coat-hanger covers as given for girl's set.
Using photograph as a guide, sew wheels to car, then sew car to coat hanger just below hook.

# rabbit case

• • • • • • • • •

This cute rabbit case is very versatile, with its stripy body, little legs, and quizzical face. It is crocheted in Rowan *RYC Cashsoft* in a range of harmonizing and gentle tones.

Designed as a diaper holder, it can convert just as easily into a pajama case for an older child. And what small child could resist it?

It takes a bit longer to crochet than some of the other projects in this book, but will suit intermediate crocheters wanting to practice their new-found skills.

*gallery of projects*

## Size

Finished case is 11in/28cm wide, 5½in/14cm deep and 19½in/50cm tall, excluding ears.

## Yarns

2 x 50g/1¾oz balls of Rowan *RYC Cashsoft DK* in **A** (Donkey 517) and 1 ball in **F** (Savannah 507)
1 x 50g/1¾oz ball of Rowan *RYC Cashsoft Baby DK* in each of **B** (Chicory 804), **D** (Cloud 805), and **G** (Horseradish 801)
1 x 50g/1¾oz ball of Rowan *RYC Cashsoft 4 ply* in each of **C** (Monet 423) and **E** (Rose Lake 421)

## Hooks

Size G-6 (4mm) crochet hook

## Extras

Piece of firm cardboard approximately 6in/15cm by 11¾in/30cm
Washable toy filling

## Gauge

20 sts and 12 rows to 4in/10cm measured over patt using size G-6 (4mm) hook *or size to obtain correct gauge.*

## Abbreviations

**dc2tog** = [yo and insert hook in next st, yo and draw loop through, yo and draw through 2 loops] twice, yo and draw through all 3 loops on hook. See also page 117.

## Base (make 2)

Using size G-6 (4mm) hook and A, ch 57.
**Row 1 (RS)** 1 sc in 2nd ch from hook, 1 sc in each ch to end, turn. 56 sts.

**Row 2** Ch 1 (does NOT count as st), 1 sc in each sc to end, turn.

Rep row 2 until base measures 5½in/14cm.

Fasten off.

### Back

Using size G-6 (4mm) hook and A, ch 58.

**Foundation row (WS)** 1 sc in 2nd ch from hook, *ch 1, skip 1 ch, 1 sc in next ch, rep from * to end, turn. 57 sts.

Join in and breaking off colors as required, cont in patt as foll:

**Row 1 (RS)** Using B, ch 3 (does NOT count as st), skip sc at base of 3 ch, 1 dc in next ch sp, *ch 1, dc2tog inserting first "leg" in same ch sp as used for last st and second "leg" in next ch sp, rep from * to end, working second "leg" of last dc2tog in sc at beg of previous row, turn.

**Row 2** Using C, ch 1 (does NOT count as st), skip dc2tog at end of last row, 1 sc in first ch sp, *ch 1, skip 1 dc2tog, 1 sc in next ch sp, rep from * until sc has been worked in last ch sp, turn. 55 sts.

**Row 3** Using D, as row 1.

**Row 4** Using E, as row 2. 53 sts.

**Row 5** Using A, as row 1.

**Row 6** Using B, as row 2. 51 sts.

**Row 7** Using C, as row 1.

**Row 8** Using D, as row 2. 49 sts.

**Row 9** Using E, as row 1.

**Row 10** Using A, as row 2. 47 sts.

These 10 rows form patt and start shaping.

Keeping stripes correct as set, cont as foll:

**Rows 11 to 32** As rows 1 and 2, 11 times. 25 sts.

**Row 33** As row 1. (This row should have been worked using D.)

**Place markers at both ends of last row.

Keeping stripes correct as set, now shape upper edge as foll:

**Row 34 (WS)** Slip st across and in 2nd ch sp, ch 1 (does NOT count as st), 1 sc in same ch sp, *ch 1, skip 1 dc2tog, 1 sc in next ch sp, rep from * until sc has been worked in last-but-one ch sp, turn. 19 sts.

**Row 35** Ch 3 (does NOT count as st), skip sc at base of 3 ch, 1 dc in next ch sp, *ch 1, dc2tog inserting first "leg" in same ch sp as used for last st and second "leg" in next ch sp, rep from * to end, working second "leg" of last dc2tog in sc at beg of previous row, turn.

**Rows 36 and 37** As rows 34 and 35. 13 sts.

Fasten off.

### Front

Work as given for back until row 3 has been completed, ending with RS facing for next row. 55 sts.

**DIVIDE FOR FRONT OPENING**

Keeping stripes correct as set by back, cont as foll:

**Row 4** Ch 1 (does NOT count as st), skip dc2tog at end of last row, 1 sc in first ch sp, [ch 1, skip 1 dc2tog, 1 sc in next ch sp] 11 times, turn, leaving rem sts unworked. 23 sts.

**Row 5** As row 1.

**Row 6** Ch 1 (does NOT count as st), skip dc2tog at end of last row, 1 sc in first ch sp, *ch 1, skip 1 dc2tog, 1 sc in next ch sp, rep from * until sc has been worked in last ch sp, 1 sc in next dc, turn. 22 sts.

**Row 7** Ch 3 (counts as first dc), dc2tog inserting first "leg" in sc at base of 3 ch and second "leg" in first ch sp, *ch 1, dc2tog inserting first "leg" in same ch sp as used for last st and second "leg" in next ch sp, rep from * to end, working second "leg" of last dc2tog in sc at beg of previous row, turn.

**Row 8** Ch 1 (does NOT count as st), skip dc2tog at end of last row, 1 sc in first ch sp, *ch 1, skip 1 dc2tog, 1 sc in next ch sp, rep from * until sc has been worked in last ch sp, ch 1, skip 1 dc2tog, 1 sc in top of 3 ch at beg of previous row, turn. 21 sts.

**Rows 9 to 28** As rows 5 to 8, 5 times. 11 sts.

**Rows 29 to 31** As rows 5 to 7. 10 sts.
Fasten off.

Return to last complete row worked. With WS facing, using appropriate color yarn and keeping stripes correct as set by back, cont as foll:

**Row 4** Skip 3 ch sps after first side, rejoin yarn in next ch sp, ch 1 (does NOT count as st), 1 sc in same ch sp as where yarn was rejoined, [ch 1, skip 1 dc2tog, 1 sc in next ch sp] 11 times, turn. 23 sts.

**Row 5** As row 1.

**Row 6** Ch 1 (does NOT count as st), 1 sc in dc2tog at end of last row, 1 sc in first ch sp, *ch 1, skip 1 dc2tog, 1 sc in next ch sp, rep from * until sc has been worked in last ch sp, turn. 22 sts.

**Row 7** Ch 3 (does NOT count as st), 1 dc in first ch sp, *ch 1, dc2tog inserting first "leg" in same ch sp as used for last st and second "leg" in next ch sp, rep from * to end, working second "leg" of last dc2tog in sc at beg of previous row, 1 dc in sc at base of second "leg" of last dc2tog, turn.

**Row 8** Ch 1 (does NOT count as st), 1 sc in dc at end of previous row, *ch 1, skip 1 dc2tog, 1 sc in next ch sp, rep from * until sc has been worked in last ch sp, turn. 21 sts.

**Rows 9 to 28** As rows 5 to 8, 5 times. 11 sts.

**Rows 29 to 31** As rows 5 to 7. 10 sts.
Fasten off.

**JOIN SECTIONS**

With WS facing, using appropriate color yarn and keeping stripes correct as set by back, cont as foll:

**Row 32** Attach yarn to first ch sp of row 31 of first section, ch 1 (does NOT count as st), 1 sc in same ch sp, [ch 1, skip 1 dc2tog, 1 sc in next ch sp] 3 times, ch 1, skip 1 dc2tog, 1 sc in top of 3 ch at beg of row 31 of first section, ch 7, 1 sc in dc at end of row 31 of second section, [ch 1, skip 1 dc2tog, 1 sc in next ch sp] 4 times, turn. 25 sts.

**Row 33** Ch 3 (does NOT count as st), skip sc at base of 3 ch, 1 dc in next ch sp, [ch 1, dc2tog inserting first "leg" in same ch sp as used for last st and second "leg" in next ch sp] 3 times, ch 1, dc2tog inserting first "leg" in same ch sp as used for last st, skip 1 sc and work second "leg" in next ch, [ch 1, dc2tog inserting first "leg" in same ch as used for last st, skip 1 ch and work second "leg" in next ch] 3 times, ch 1, dc2tog inserting first "leg" in same ch as used for last st, skip 1 sc and work second "leg" in next ch sp, [ch 1, dc2tog inserting first "leg" in same ch sp as used for last st and second "leg" in next ch sp] 3 times, ch 1, dc2tog inserting first "leg" in same ch sp as used for last st and second "leg" in sc at beg of previous row, turn.

Complete as given for back from **.

**Sides** (make 2)

Using size G-6 (4mm) hook and A, ch 30.

Work foundation row as given for back. 29 sts.

Join in and breaking off colors as required, cont in patt as foll:

**Row 1 (RS)** Using B, ch 3 (does NOT count as st), skip sc at base of 3 ch, 1 dc in next ch sp, *ch 1, dc2tog inserting first "leg" in same ch sp as used for last st and second "leg" in next ch sp, rep from * to end, working second "leg" of last dc2tog in sc at beg of previous row, turn.

**Row 2** Using C, ch 1 (does NOT count as st), skip dc2tog at end of last row, 1 sc in first ch sp, *ch 1, skip 1 dc2tog, 1 sc in next ch sp, rep from * until sc has been worked in last ch sp, turn. 27 sts.

**Row 3** Using D, as row 1.

**Row 4** Using E, ch 1 (does NOT count as st), 1 sc in dc2tog at end of previous row, 1 sc in next ch sp, *ch 1, skip 1 dc2tog, 1 sc in next ch sp, rep from * until sc has been worked in last ch sp, 1 sc in next dc, turn.

**Row 5** Using A, ch 3 (does NOT count as st), skip sc at base of 3 ch and next sc, 1 dc in next ch sp, *ch 1, dc2tog inserting first "leg" in same ch sp as used for last st and second "leg" in next ch sp, rep from * to end, working second "leg" of last dc2tog in first sc of previous row, turn. 25 sts.

**Row 6** Using B, as row 4.

**Row 7** Using C, ch 3 (counts as 1 dc), skip sc at base of 3 ch, dc2tog inserting first "leg" in sc at base of 3 ch and second "leg" in first ch sp, *ch 1, dc2tog inserting first "leg" in same ch sp as used for last st and second "leg" in next ch sp, rep from * to end, working second "leg" of last dc2tog in first sc of previous row, 1 dc in same sc as used for second "leg" of last dc2tog, turn.

**Row 8** Using D, ch 1 (does NOT count as st), 1 sc in dc at end of previous row, *ch 1, skip 1 dc2tog, 1 sc in next ch sp, rep from * to end, working last sc in top of 3 ch at beg of previous row, turn.

These 10 rows set position of patt as for back and start shaping.

Keeping stripes correct as set by back, cont as foll:

**Rows 9 to 15** As rows 1 to 7. 21 sts.

**Row 16** Ch 1 (does NOT count as st), skip dc at end of previous row, 1 sc in next dc2tog, 1 sc in next ch sp, *ch 1, skip 1 dc2tog, 1 sc in next ch sp, rep from * until sc has been worked in last ch sp, 1 sc in next dc2tog, turn, leaving 3 ch at beg of previous row unworked. 19 sts.

**Row 17** As row 7.

**Rows 18 to 31** As rows 16 and 17, 7 times. 5 sts.

**Row 32** As row 16. 3 sts.

**Row 33** Ch 3 (does NOT count as st), skip sc at base of 3 ch, dc2tog over next 2 sc.

Fasten off.

## Head

Using size G-6 (4mm) hook and F, ch 2.

**Round 1 (RS)** 8 sc in 2nd ch from hook, 1 slip st in first sc, turn. 8 sts.

**Round 2** Ch 1 (does NOT count as st), 2 sc in each sc to end, 1 slip st in first sc, turn. 16 sts.

**Round 3** Ch 1 (does NOT count as st), [1 sc in next sc, 2 sc in next sc] 8 times, 1 slip st in first sc, turn. 24 sts.

**Round 4** Ch 1 (does NOT count as st), 2 sc in first sc, 1 sc in each of next 10 sc, 2 sc in each of next 2 sc, 1 sc in each of next 10 sc, 2 sc in last sc, 1 slip st in first sc, turn. 28 sts.

**Round 5** Ch 1 (does NOT count as st), 2 sc in first sc, 1 sc in each of next 12 sc, 2 sc in each of next 2 sc, 1 sc in each of next 12 sc, 2 sc in last sc, 1 slip st in first sc, turn. 32 sts.

**Round 6** Ch 1 (does NOT count as st), 1 sc in each of first 15 sc, 2 sc in each of next 2 sc, 1 sc in each of last 15 sc, 1 slip st in first sc, turn. 34 sts.

**Round 7** Ch 1 (does NOT count as st), 2 sc in first sc, 1 sc in each of next 15 sc, 2 sc in each of next 2 sc, 1 sc in each of next 15 sc, 2 sc in last sc, 1 slip st in first sc, turn. 38 sts.

**Round 8** Ch 1 (does NOT count as st), 1 sc in each of first 18 sc, 2 sc in each of next 2 sc, 1 sc in each of last 18 sc, 1 slip st in first sc, turn. 40 sts.

**Round 9** Ch 1 (does NOT count as st), 2 sc in first sc, 1 sc in each of next 18 sc, 2 sc in each of next 2 sc, 1 sc in each of next 18 sc, 2 sc in last sc, 1 slip st in first sc, turn. 44 sts.

**Round 10** Ch 1 (does NOT count as st), 1 sc in each of first 21 sc, 2 sc in each of next 2 sc, 1 sc in each of last 21 sc, 1 slip st in first sc, turn. 46 sts.

**Round 11** Ch 1 (does NOT count as st), 1 sc in each of first 22 sc, 2 sc in each of next 2 sc, 1 sc in each of last 22 sc, 1 slip st in first sc, turn. 48 sts.

**Round 12** Ch 1 (does NOT count as st), 1 sc in each st to end, 1 slip st in first sc, turn.

**Rounds 13 to 20** As round 12.

**Round 21** Ch 1 (does NOT count as st), sc2tog over first 2 sc, 1 sc in each of next 20 sc, [sc2tog over next 2 sc] twice, 1 sc in each of next 20 sc, sc2tog over last 2 sc, 1 slip st in first sc, turn. 44 sts.

**Round 22** Ch 1 (does NOT count as st), 1 sc in each of first 20 sts, [sc2tog over next 2 sc] twice, 1 sc in each of last 20 sts, 1 slip st in first sc, turn. 42 sts.

**Round 23** Ch 1 (does NOT count as st), 1 sc in each of first 19 sts, [sc2tog over next 2 sc] twice, 1 sc in each of last

19 sts, 1 slip st in first sc, turn. 40 sts.

**Round 24** Ch 1 (does NOT count as st), sc2tog over first 2 sc, 1 sc in each of next 14 sc, [sc2tog over next 2 sc] 4 times, 1 sc in each of next 14 sc, sc2tog over last 2 sc, 1 slip st in first sc, turn. 34 sts.

**Round 25** Ch 1 (does NOT count as st), 1 sc in each of first 13 sts, [sc2tog over next 2 sc] 4 times, 1 sc in each of last 13 sts, 1 slip st in first sc, turn. 30 sts.

**Round 26** Ch 1 (does NOT count as st), 1 sc in each of first 13 sts, [sc2tog over next 2 sc] twice, 1 sc in each of last 13 sts, 1 slip st in first sc, turn. 28 sts.

**Round 27** Ch 1 (does NOT count as st), sc2tog over first 2 sc, 1 sc in each of next 10 sc, [sc2tog over next 2 sc] twice, 1 sc in each of next 10 sc, sc2tog over last 2 sc, 1 slip st in first sc, turn. 24 sts.

**Round 28** As round 12.
Break off F and join in G.

**Round 29** Ch 1 (does NOT count as st), working into front loops only of sts of previous round: 1 sc in each sc to end, 1 slip st in first sc, turn.

**Round 30** As round 12.

**Round 31** Ch 1 (does NOT count as st), 1 sc in each of first 17 sc, ch 18, skip 1 sc, 1 sc in each of last 6 sc, 1 slip st in first sc, turn. 41 sts.

**Round 32** Ch 1 (does NOT count as st), 1 sc in each of first 6 sc, 1 sc in each of next 18 ch, 1 sc in each of last 17 sc, 1 slip st in first sc, turn.

**Round 33** Ch 1 (does NOT count as st), 1 sc in each of first 17 sc, 1 dc in sc skipped on round 30 enclosing ch and sc loop in st, skip ch and sc loop, 1 sc in each of last 6 sc, 1 slip st in first sc, turn. 24 sts.

**Round 34** As round 12.

**Round 35** Ch 1 (does NOT count as st), picking up corresponding back loops of sts of round 28 at same time, 1 sc in each st to end, 1 slip st in first sc, turn.
Insert toy filling in Head so that it is firmly filled.

**Round 36** Ch 1 (does NOT count as st), [1 sc in next sc, sc2tog over next 2 sc] 8 times, 1 slip st in first sc, turn. 16 sts.

**Round 37** Ch 1 (does NOT count as st), [sc2tog over next 2 sts] 8 times, 1 slip st in first sc, turn. 8 sts.

**Round 38** Ch 1 (does NOT count as st), [sc2tog over next 2 sts] 4 times, 1 slip st in first sc.
Fasten off.

**Arms** (make 2)
Using size G-6 (4mm) hook and F, ch 2.

**Round 1 (RS)** 8 sc in 2nd ch from hook, 1 slip st in first sc, turn. 8 sts.

**Round 2** Ch 1 (does NOT count as st), [1 sc in next sc, 2 sc in next sc] 4 times, 1 slip st in first sc, turn. 12 sts.

**Round 3** Ch 1 (does NOT count as st), [1 sc in each of next 2 sc, 2 sc in next sc] 4 times, 1 slip st in first sc, turn. 16 sts.

**Round 4** Ch 1 (does NOT count as st), 1 sc in each sc to end, 1 slip st in first sc, turn.

**Rounds 5 and 6** As round 4.

**Round 7** Ch 1 (does NOT count as st), [sc2tog over next 2 sc, 1 sc in each of next 2 sc] 4 times, 1 slip st in first sc2tog, turn. 12 sts.

**Round 8** Ch 1 (does NOT count as st), [sc2tog over next 2 sc] 6 times, 1 slip st in first sc2tog, turn. 6 sts.

**Round 9** Ch 1 (does NOT count as st), 2 sc in each st to end, 1 slip st in first sc, turn. 12 sts.

**Rounds 10 to 22** As round 4.
Fasten off.

**Legs** (make 2)
Using size G-6 (4mm) hook and A, ch 4.

**Round 1 (RS)** 2 sc in 2nd ch from hook, 1 sc in next ch, 4 sc in last ch, working back along foundation ch edge: 1 sc in next sc, 2 sc in same ch as first 2 sc, 1 slip st in first sc, turn. 10 sts.

**Round 2** Ch 1 (does NOT count as st), 2 sc in each sc to end, 1 slip st in first sc, turn. 20 sts.

**Round 3** Ch 1 (does NOT count as st), 1 sc in each sc to end, 1 slip st in first sc, turn.

**Rounds 4 and 5** As round 3.

**Round 6** Ch 1 (does NOT count as st), 1 sc in each of first 8 sc, [sc2tog over next 2 sc] twice, 1 sc in each of last 8 sc, 1 slip st in first sc, turn. 18 sts.

**Round 7** Ch 1 (does NOT count as st), 1 sc in each of first 7 sc, [sc2tog over next 2 sc] twice, 1 sc in each of last 7 sc, 1 slip st in first sc, turn. 16 sts.

**Round 8** Ch 1 (does NOT count as st), 1 sc in each of first 4 sc, [sc2tog over next 2 sc] 4 times, 1 sc in each of last 4 sc, 1 slip st in first sc, turn. 12 sts.
Break off A and join in E.

**Round 9** Ch 1 (does NOT count as st), working in front loops only of sts of previous round: 1 sc in each sc to end, 1 slip st in first sc, turn.

**LEFT LEG ONLY**

**Round 10** Ch 1 (does NOT count as st), 1 sc in each of first 8 sc, ch 14, skip 1 sc, 1 sc in each of last 3 sc, 1 slip st in first sc, turn. 25 sts.

**Round 11** Ch 1 (does NOT count as st), 1 sc in each of first 3 sc, 1 sc in each of next 14 ch, 1 sc in each of last 8 sc, 1 slip st in first sc, turn.

**Round 12** Ch 1 (does NOT count as st), 1 sc in each of first 8 sc, 1 dc in sc skipped on round 10 enclosing ch and sc loop in st, skip ch and sc loop, 1 sc in each of last 3 sc, 1 slip st in first sc, turn.

**RIGHT LEG ONLY**

**Round 10** Ch 1 (does NOT count as st), 1 sc in each of first 3 sc, ch 14, skip 1 sc, 1 sc in each of last 8 sc, 1 slip st in first sc, turn. 25 sts.

**Round 11** Ch 1 (does NOT count as st), 1 sc in each of first 8 sc, 1 sc in each of next 14 ch, 1 sc in each of last 3 sc, 1 slip st in first sc, turn.

**Round 12** Ch 1 (does NOT count as st), 1 sc in each of first 3 sc, 1 dc in sc skipped on round 10 enclosing ch and sc loop in st, skip ch and sc loop, 1 sc in each of last 8 sc, 1 slip st in first sc, turn.

**BOTH LEGS**

Break off E and join in F.

**Round 13** Ch 1 (does NOT count as st), picking up corresponding back loops of sts of round 9 at same time, 1 sc in each st to end, 1 slip st in first sc, turn. 12 sts.

**Rounds 14 to 24** As round 3. Fasten off.

**Inner ears** (make 2)

Using size G-6 (4mm) hook and G, ch 15.

**Row 1 (RS)** 1 sc in 2nd ch from hook, 1 sc in each of next 12 ch, 5 sc in last ch, working back along other side of foundation ch 1 sc in each of next 13 ch, turn. 31 sts.

**Row 2** Ch 1 (does NOT count as st), 1 sc in each of first 4 sc, 1 hdc in each of next 4 sc, 1 dc in each of next 3 sc, 1 hdc in each of next 2 sc, 1 sc in each of next 2 sc, 3 sc in next sc, 1 sc in each of next 2 sc, 1 hdc in each of next 2 sc, 1 dc in each of next 3 sc, 1 hdc in each of next 4 sc, 1 sc in each of last 4 sc, turn. 33 sts.

**Row 3** Ch 1 (does NOT count as st), 1 sc in each of first 16 sts, 3 sc in next sc, 1 sc in each of last 16 sc. Fasten off.

**Outer ears** (make 2)

Using F, work as for Inner Ears to end of row 3, turn.

**Row 4** Ch 1 (does NOT count as st), 1 sc in each sc to end, turn.

Holding Inner Ear against RS of Outer Ear, rep last row once more, working each st through sts of both Ear pieces. Fasten off. Turn completed Ear RS out.

**Finishing**

Press lightly on WS following instructions on yarn label.

**FRONT OPENING EDGINGS** (both alike)

With RS facing, using size G-6 (4mm) hook and A, attach yarn at base of right side of front opening, ch 1 (does NOT count as st), work in sc evenly up row-end edge of opening to top of opening, turn.

**Next row (WS)** Ch 1 (does NOT count as st), 1 sc in each sc to end, turn.

Break off A and join in B.

Rep last row once more. Fasten off.

Work edging along other side of opening in same way, but starting at top of opening. Sew row-end edges of edgings in place at top and bottom of opening, ensuring edgings meet at center.

Matching foundation ch edges and markers on Back and Front to fasten-off point of Sides, sew Sides to Back and Front below markers. Join front and back above markers, leaving top of last row open.

Insert toy filling in Arms, then flatten top of last round and sew top edge closed. Using photograph as a guide, sew top edge of Arms to Front and Back seam above markers.

Sew base of Head to top of Back and Front. Fold Ears flat and sew row-end edges closed, making a small pleat. Sew Ears to Head.

**NOSE**

Using size G-6 (4mm) hook and A, make 2ch.

**Round 1 (RS)** 4 sc in to 2nd ch from hook, 1 slip st in first sc. 4 sts.

**Round 2** Ch 1 (does NOT count as st), [1 sc in next sc, 2 sc in next sc] twice, 1 slip st in first sc. 6 sts.

**Round 3** Ch 1 (does NOT count as st), 1 sc in each sc to end, 1 slip st in first sc.

Fasten off, leaving a long end.

Insert scrap of filling in Nose. Then using photograph as a guide, sew Nose to face and embroider eyes using A.

Sew one Base piece to lower edges of Front, Back and Sides. Now sew second Base piece in place over first, leaving back edge open. Trim piece of cardboard to fit base and slip between base pieces, so it is removable for washing.)

Insert toy filling in Legs. Sew top edge of Legs to Base.

**HANGING LOOP**

Using size G-6 (4mm) hook and F, ch 21.

**Row 1 (RS)** 1 sc in 2nd ch from hook, 1 sc in each ch to end. Fasten off.

Fold hanging loop in half and attach ends to top of Head.

# cushion and blanket

• • • • • • • • •

This pretty crochet cushion and blanket set can be crocheted in the pink colorway shown or in the alternative blues colorway.

Worked in Rowan's beautifully soft *RYC Cashsoft* yarn, the cushion and blanket are made with the same basic design. With different patchwork squares and rectangles to work in different stitch patterns, they are perfect projects for any intermediate-level crocheter who wants a challenge.

The blanket comes in two sizes: a smaller stroller blanket and a larger crib blanket. As with the cushion, the heart motifs are made separately and appliquéd onto the base, and a lacy border edges the designs beautifully.

# cushion

## Size
Finished cushion cover fits 18in/46cm square pillow form.

## Yarns
2 x 50g/1¾oz balls of Rowan *RYC Cashsoft DK* in each of **A**
(Donkey 517) and **C** (Cream 500)
1 x 50g/1¾oz ball of Rowan *RYC Cashsoft DK* in **B** (Bloom 520
or Ballad Blue 508)
3 x 50g/1¾oz balls of Rowan *RYC Cashsoft Baby DK* in **D**
(Pixie 807 or Chicory 804)
2 x 50g/1¾oz balls of Rowan *RYC Cashsoft 4 ply* in **E** (Rose
Lake 421 or Spa 424)

## Hook
Size G-6 (4mm) crochet hook

## Extras
18in/46cm square pillow form

## Gauge
First 6 rounds of panel A measure 4¾in/12cm square using
size G-6 (4mm) hook *or size to obtain correct gauge.*

## Abbreviations
**sc3tog** = [insert hook in next st, yo and draw loop through] 3
times, yo and draw through all 4 loops on hook; **dc2tog** = [yo
and insert hook in next st, yo and draw loop through, yo and
draw through 2 loops] twice, yo and draw through all 3 loops
on hook; **dc3tog** = [yo and insert hook in next st, yo and draw
loop through, yo and draw through 2 loops] 3 times, yo and
draw through all 4 loops on hook; **dc4tog** = [yo and insert
hook in next st, yo and draw loop through, yo and draw
through 2 loops] 4 times, yo and draw through all 5 loops on
hook; **dc7tog** = [yo and insert hook in next st, yo and draw

loop through, yo and draw through 2 loops] 7 times, yo and
draw through all 8 loops on hook.
See also page 117.

## Panel A (make 2)
Using size G-6 (4mm) hook and D, ch 4 and join with a slip st
to first ch to make a ring.
**Round 1 (RS)** Ch 5 (counts as 1 dc and 2 ch), [3 dc in ring, ch
2] 3 times, 2 dc in ring, 1 slip st in 3rd of 5 ch at beg of round.
**Round 2** Slip st in first (corner) ch sp, ch 7 (counts as 1 dc
and 4 ch), 2 dc in same ch sp, *1 dc in each of next 3 dc**,
[2 dc, ch 4 and 2 dc] in next (corner) ch sp, rep from * to end,
ending last rep at **, 1 dc in same ch sp as used for slip st at
beg of round, 1 slip st in 3rd of 7 ch at beg of round.
**Round 3** Slip st in first (corner) ch sp, ch 7 (counts as 1 dc and
4 ch), 2 dc in same ch sp, *1 dc in each of next 7 dc**, [2 dc,
ch 4 and 2 dc] in next (corner) ch sp, rep from * to end,
ending last rep at **, 1 dc in same ch sp as used for slip st at
beg of round, 1 slip st in 3rd of 7 ch at beg of round.
Break off D and join in E.
**Round 4** Slip st in first (corner) ch sp, ch 7 (counts as 1 dc and
4 ch), 2 dc in same ch sp, *1 dc in each of next 11 dc**, [2 dc,
ch 4 and 2 dc] in next (corner) ch sp, rep from * to end,
ending last rep at **, 1 dc in same ch sp as used for slip st at
beg of round, 1 slip st in 3rd of 7 ch at beg of round.
**Round 5** Slip st in first (corner) ch sp, ch 7 (counts as 1 dc and
4 ch), 2 dc in same ch sp, *1 dc in each of next 15 dc**, [2 dc,
ch 4 and 2 dc] in next (corner) ch sp, rep from * to end,
ending last rep at **, 1 dc in same ch sp as used for slip st at
beg of round, 1 slip st in 3rd of 7 ch at beg of round.
Fasten off E and join in A to one corner ch sp.
**Round 6** Ch 1 (does NOT count as st), 3 sc in corner ch sp
where yarn was rejoined, *1 sc in each of next 19 sc**, 6 sc in
next corner ch sp, rep from * to end, ending last rep at **, 3 sc
in same corner ch sp as used for first 3 sc, 1 slip st in first sc.
Break off A and join in C.

**Round 7** Ch 4 (counts as 1 dc and 1 ch), 1 dc in sc at base of 4 ch, *[ch 1, skip 1 sc, 1 dc in next sc] 12 times, ch 1, skip 1 sc**, [1 dc, ch 1, 1 dc, ch 1 and 1 dc] in next sc, rep from * to end, ending last rep at **, 1 dc in sc at base of 4 ch at beg of round, ch 1, 1 slip st in 3rd of 4 ch at beg of round.
Break off C and join in D.

**Round 8** Ch 4 (counts as 1 dc and 1 ch), 1 dc in st at base of 4 ch, *ch 1, [1 dc in next ch sp, ch 1, skip 1 dc] 14 times, 1 dc in next ch sp, ch 1**, [1 dc, ch 1, 1 dc, ch 1 and 1 dc] in next dc, rep from * to end, ending last rep at **, 1 dc in st at base of 4 ch at beg of round, ch 1, 1 slip st in 3rd of 4 ch at beg of round.
Break off D and join in E.

**Round 9** Ch 3 (counts as 1 dc), 1 dc in st at base of 3 ch, *ch 1, 1 dc in next ch sp, [1 dc in next dc, ch 1, skip 1 ch, 1 dc in next dc, 1 dc in next ch sp, ch 1, skip 1 dc, 1 dc in next ch sp] 5 times, 1 dc in next dc, ch 1, skip 1 ch, 1 dc in next dc, 1 dc in next ch sp, ch 1**, 3 dc in next dc, rep from * to end, ending last rep at **, 1 dc in st at base of 3 ch at beg of round, 1 slip st in top of 3 ch at beg of round.
Break off E and join in B.

**Round 10** Ch 4 (counts as 1 dc and 1 ch), 1 dc in st at base of 4 ch, *[1 dc in next dc, ch 1, skip 1 ch, 1 dc in next dc] 13 times**, [1 dc, ch 1, 1 dc, ch 1 and 1 dc] in next dc, rep from * to end, ending last rep at **, 1 dc in st at base of 4 ch at beg of round, ch 1, 1 slip st in 3rd of 4 ch at beg of round.
Break off B and join in A.

**Round 11** Ch 1 (does NOT count as st), 3 sc in st at base of 1 ch, *[1 sc in next ch sp, 1 sc in each of next 2 dc] 14 times, 1 sc in next ch sp**, 3 sc in next dc, rep from * to end, ending last rep at **, 1 slip st in first sc.
Fasten off.

**Panel B** (make 8)
Work as given for panel A to end of round 6.
Fasten off.

**Panel C** (make 4)
Using size G-6 (4mm) hook and D, ch 30.
**Row 1 (RS)** 1 dc in 6th ch from hook, *skip 2 ch, 5 dc in next ch, skip 2 ch, 1 dc in next ch, ch 1, skip 1 ch, 1 dc in next ch, rep from * to end, turn. 3 patt reps.
**Row 2** Ch 4 (counts as 1 dc and 1 ch), skip dc at base of 4 ch and next ch, 1 dc in next dc, *skip 2 dc, 5 dc in next dc, skip 2 dc, 1 dc in next dc, ch 1, skip 1 ch, 1 dc in next dc, rep from * to end, working last dc in 3rd of 4 ch at beg of previous row, turn.
Rep row 2 until side panel fits along edge of center square (Panel A), ending with RS facing for next row.
Break off D and join in A.
**Edging round (RS)** Ch 1 (does NOT count as st), 2 sc in st at base of 1 ch, 1 sc in next ch sp, [1 sc in each of next 7 dc, skip 1 ch] twice, 1 sc in each of next 7 dc, 1 sc in next ch sp, 3 sc in 3rd of 4 ch at beg of previous row, work 43 sc evenly down row-end edge to foundation ch edge, 3 sc in first (corner) foundation ch, 1 sc in next foundation ch, [1 sc in each of next 7 ch, skip 1 ch] twice, 1 sc in each of next 8 ch, 3 sc in next (corner) ch, work 43 sc evenly up other row-end edge, 1 sc in same place as 2 sc at beg of round, 1 slip st in first sc.
Fasten off.

**Panel D** (make 4)
Using size G-6 (4mm) hook and E, ch 47.
**Row 1 (RS)** 1 sc in 2nd ch from hook, 1 sc in next ch, *skip 3 ch**, 7 dc in next ch, skip 3 ch, 1 sc in each of next 3 ch, rep from * to end, ending last rep at **, 4 dc in last ch, turn. 4½ patt reps.
Join in C.
**Row 2** Using C, ch 1 (does NOT count as st), 1 sc in each of first 2 dc, *ch 3**, dc7tog over next 7 sts, ch 3, 1 sc in each of next 3 dc, rep from * to end, ending last rep at **, dc4tog over last 4 sts, turn.

*gallery of projects*

**Row 3** Using C, ch 3 (counts as first dc), 3 dc in st at base of 3 ch, *skip 3 ch**, 1 sc in each of next 3 sc, skip 3 ch, 7 dc in next dc7tog, rep from * to end, ending last rep at **, 1 sc in each of last 2 sc, turn.

**Row 4** Using E, ch 3 (does NOT count as st), skip sc at base of 3 ch, dc3tog over next 3 sts, *ch 3**, 1 sc in each of next 3 dc, ch 3, dc7tog over next 7 sts, rep from * to end, ending last rep at **, 1 sc in next dc, 1 sc in top of 3 ch at beg of previous row, turn.

**Row 5** Using E, ch 1 (does NOT count as st), 1 sc in each of first 2 sc, *skip 3 ch**, 7 dc in next dc7tog, skip 3 ch, 1 sc in each of next 3 sc, rep from * to end, ending last rep at **, 4 dc in dc3tog at beg of previous row, turn.

**Rows 6 to 9** As rows 2 to 5.

**Rows 10 to 12** As rows 2 to 4.

Break off E and join in A.

**Edging round (RS)** Ch 1 (does NOT count as st), 2 sc in st at base of 1 ch, 1 sc in next sc, 2 sc in next ch sp, [1 sc in next dc7tog, 3 sc in next ch sp, 1 sc in each of next 3 sc, 3 sc in next ch sp] 4 times, 3 sc in dc3tog at beg of previous row, work 23 sc evenly down row-end edge to foundation ch edge, 3 sc in first (corner) foundation ch, [3 sc in next ch sp, 1 sc in each of next 3 ch, 3 sc in next ch sp, 1 sc in next ch] 4 times, 2 sc in next ch sp, 1 sc in next ch, 3 sc in next (corner) ch, work 23 sc evenly up other row-end edge, 1 sc in same place as 2 sc at beg of round, 1 slip st in first sc.

Fasten off.

**Hearts** (make 10)

Using size G-6 (4mm) hook and B, ch 2.

**Row 1 (RS)** 3 sc in 2nd ch from hook, turn. 3 sts.

**Row 2** Ch 1 (does NOT count as st), 2 sc in first sc, 1 sc in next sc, 2 sc in last sc, turn. 5 sts.

**Row 3** Ch 1 (does NOT count as st), 2 sc in first sc, 1 sc in each of next 3 sc, 2 sc in last sc, turn. 7 sts.

**Row 4** Ch 1 (does NOT count as st), 1 sc in each sc to end, turn.

**Row 5** Ch 1 (does NOT count as st), 2 sc in first sc, 1 sc in each of next 5 sc, 2 sc in last sc, turn. 9 sts.

**Row 6** As row 4.

**Row 7** Ch 1 (does NOT count as st), 2 sc in first sc, 1 sc in each of next 7 sc, 2 sc in last sc, turn. 11 sts.

**Rows 8 to 10** As row 4.

**Row 11** Ch 1 (does NOT count as st), sc2tog over first 2 sc, 1 sc in each of next 3 sc and turn, leaving rem 6 sts unworked.

**Row 12** Ch 1 (does NOT count as st), [sc2tog over next 2 sts] twice.

Fasten off.

Return to row 10, skip 1 sc at center, rejoin yarn to next sc and cont as foll:

**Row 11** Ch 1 (does NOT count as st), 1 sc in each of next 3 sc, sc2tog over last 2 sc, turn.

**Row 12** Ch 1 (does NOT count as st), [sc2tog over next 2 sts] twice.

Fasten off.

With RS facing, using size G-6 (4mm) hook and A, attach yarn to base of heart, ch 1 (does NOT count as st), 3 sc in base of heart, work in sc evenly around entire heart shape, working sc3tog at point where top sections meet and ending with 1 slip st in first sc.

Fasten off.

**Finishing**

Arrange cushion front as shown on page 98, using one Panel A, two Panel C's, two Panel D's, and four Panel B's, then sew together. Sew together remaining Panels in same way for back. Sew hearts to centers of Panels A and B.

Pin out to form a 18in/46cm square and press lightly on WS following instructions on yarn label.

**EDGING**

With RS facing, using size G-6 (4mm) hook and A, attach yarn at one corner of joined panels and cont as foll:

**Round 1 (RS)** Ch 1 (does NOT count as st), 2 sc in place where yarn was rejoined—place marker on first of these 2 sc, *work 95 sc along edge of joined panels to next corner**, 3 sc in next corner—place marker on 2nd of these 3 sc, rep from * to end, ending last rep at **, 1 sc in same place as used for first 2 sc, 1 slip st in first sc. 392 sts.
Break off A and join in C.

**Round 2** Ch 4 (counts as 1 dc and 1 ch)—place marker on 3rd of these 4 ch, 1 dc in sc at base of 4 ch, *[ch 1, skip 1 sc, 1 dc in next sc] until dc has been worked in marked sc**, [ch 1, 1 dc—place marker on this dc, ch 1 and 1 dc] in same sc as last dc, rep from * to end, ending last rep at **—last dc will have been worked in sc at base of 4 ch at beg of round, ch 1, 1 slip st in 3rd of 4 ch at beg of round.
Break off C and join in D.

**Round 3** Ch 4 (counts as 1 dc and 1 ch)—place marker on 3rd of these 4 ch, 1 dc in st at base of 4 ch, *ch 1, [1 dc in next ch sp, ch 1, skip 1 dc] until one ch sp remains before marked corner dc, 1 dc in next ch sp, ch 1**, [1 dc, ch 1, 1 dc, ch 1 and 1 dc] in next marked dc, rep from * to end, ending last rep at **, 1 dc in st at base of 4 ch at beg of round, ch 1, 1 slip st in 3rd of 4 ch at beg of round.
Break off D and join in E.

**Round 4** Ch 3 (counts as 1 dc)—place marker on 3rd of these 3 ch, 1 dc in st at base of 3 ch, *ch 1, 1 dc in next ch sp, [1 dc in next dc, ch 1, skip 1 ch, 1 dc in next dc, 1 dc in next ch sp, ch 1, skip 1 dc, 1 dc in next ch sp] until two ch sps rem before marked corner dc, 1 dc in next dc, ch 1, skip 1 ch, 1 dc in next dc, 1 dc in next ch sp, ch 1**, 3 dc in next marked dc—place marker on 2nd of these 3 dc, rep from * to end, ending last rep at **, 1 dc in st at base of 3 ch at beg of round, 1 slip st in top of 3 ch at beg of round.
Break off E and join in B.

**Round 5** Ch 4 (counts as 1 dc and 1 ch)—place marker on 3rd of these 4 ch, 1 dc in st at base of 3 ch, *[1 dc in next dc, ch 1, skip 1 ch, 1 dc in next dc] to marked corner dc**,

[1 dc, ch 1, 1 dc, ch 1 and 1 dc] in next marked dc—place marker on center dc of this group of 5 sts, rep from * to end, ending last rep at **, 1 dc in st at base of 4 ch at beg of round, ch 1, 1 slip st in 3rd of 4 ch at beg of round.
Break off B and join in A.

**Round 6** Ch 1 (does NOT count as st), 2 sc in st at base of 1 ch—place marker on first of these 2 sc, *[1 sc in next ch sp, 1 sc in each of next 2 dc] until one ch sp remains before next marked dc, 1 sc in next ch sp**, 3 sc in next dc—place marker on 2nd of these 3 sc, rep from * to end, ending last rep at **, 1 sc in same place as first sc, 1 slip st in first sc.
Break off A and join in D.

**Round 7** Ch 3 (does NOT count as st), [dc2tog, ch 2—mark this ch sp—and dc3tog] in sc at base of 3 ch, *ch 5, skip 4 sc, [dc3tog in next sc, ch 5, skip 5 sc] until 5 sc rem before marked corner sc, dc3tog in next sc, ch 5, skip 4 sc**, [dc3tog, ch 2—mark this ch sp—and dc3tog] in marked sc, rep from * to end, ending last rep at **, 1 slip st in top of first dc2tog.
Break off D and join in E.

**Round 8** Ch 8 (counts as 1 dc and 5 ch), 1 dc in 5th ch from hook, *[1 dc in corner ch sp, ch 5, 1 dc in 5th ch from hook] twice, [1 dc in next dc3tog, ch 5, 1 dc in 5th ch from hook, 1 dc in next ch sp, ch 5, 1 dc in 5th ch from hook] until 1 dc3tog remains before corner ch sp**, 1 dc in next dc3tog, ch 5, 1 dc in 5th ch from hook, rep from * to end, ending last rep at **, 1 slip st in 3rd of 8 ch at beg of round.
Fasten off.

Sew front to back around outer edge of joined panels, leaving edging free and opening along one side to insert pillow form. Insert pillow form and sew opening closed.

# blanket

## Size

Stroller blanket measures 37¾in/96cm square and crib blanket measures 51in/130cm square, including edging.

## Yarns

### STROLLER BLANKET

3 x 50g/1¾oz balls of Rowan *RYC Cashsoft DK* in each of **A** (Donkey 517) and **C** (Cream 500), and 2 balls in **B** (Bloom 520 or Ballad Blue 508)

5 x 50g/1¾oz balls of Rowan *RYC Cashsoft Baby DK* in **D** (Pixie 807 or Chicory 804)

4 x 50g/1¾oz balls of Rowan *RYC Cashsoft 4 ply* in **E** (Rose Lake 421 or Spa 424)

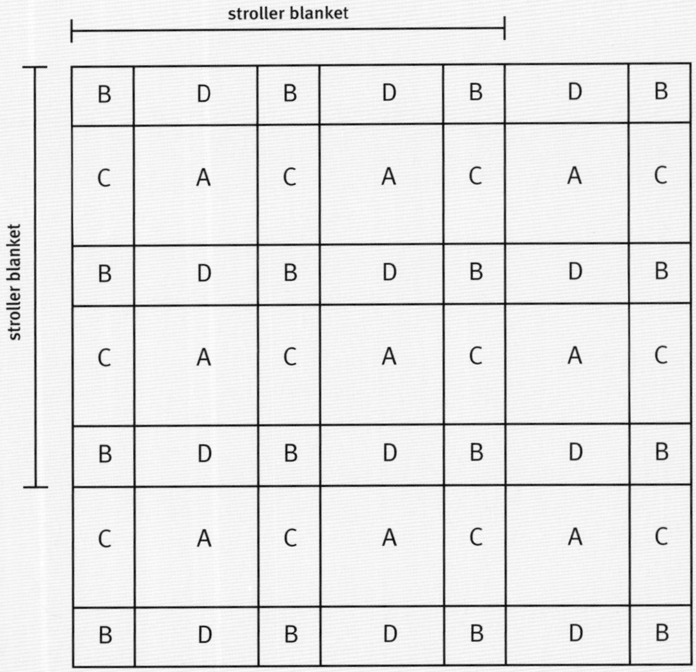

### CRIB BLANKET

5 x 50g/1¾oz balls of Rowan *RYC Cashsoft DK* in **A** (Donkey 517), 3 balls in **B** (Bloom 520 or Ballad Blue 508) and 4 balls in **C** (Cream 500)

8 x 50g/1¾oz balls of Rowan *RYC Cashsoft Baby DK* in **D** (Pixie 807 or Chicory 804)

6 x 50g/1¾oz balls of Rowan *RYC Cashsoft 4 ply* in **E** (Rose Lake 421 or Spa 424)

## Hook

Size G-6 (4mm) crochet hook

## Gauge

First 6 rounds of panel A measure 4¾in/12cm square using size G-6 (4mm) hook *or size to obtain correct gauge.*

## Abbreviations

See pages 96 and 117.

## Special note

Instructions are given for Stroller Blanket, followed by Crib Blanket in brackets [ ] in bold.

## Panels

Work 4 [9] Panel A's as for Cushion on pages 96 and 97.

Work 9 [16] Panel B's as for Cushion on page 97.

Work 6 [12] Panel C's as for Cushion on page 97.

Work 6 [12] Panel D's as for Cushion on pages 97 and 99.

**BLANKET CHART**

The chart on the left shows the arrangement of squares for both sizes of blanket. Use the whole chart for the crib blanket, and the area indicated for the smaller stroller blanket.

stroller blanket

stroller blanket

| B | D | B | D | B | D | B |
|---|---|---|---|---|---|---|
| C | A | C | A | C | A | C |
| B | D | B | D | B | D | B |
| C | A | C | A | C | A | C |
| B | D | B | D | B | D | B |
| C | A | C | A | C | A | C |
| B | D | B | D | B | D | B |

### Hearts

Work 13 [25] Hearts as for Cushion on page 99.

### Finishing

Following diagram and using A, join panels to form one large square. Attach hearts to centers of Panels A and B.

#### EDGING

With RS facing, using size G-6 (4mm) hook and A, attach yarn at one corner of joined panels and cont as foll:

**Round 1 (RS)** Ch 1 (does NOT count as st), 2 sc in place where yarn was rejoined—place marker on first of these 2 sc, *work 167 [239] sc along edge of joined panels to next corner**, 3 sc in next corner—place marker on 2nd of these 3 sc, rep from * to end, ending last rep at **, 1 sc in same place as used for first 2 sc, 1 slip st in first sc. 680 [968] sts.

Break off A and join in C.

Complete as given for edging of Cushion from beg of round 2 on page 101.

Press lightly on WS following instructions on yarn label.

# bottle covers

● ● ● ● ● ● ● ● ●

Not only do these little crochet covers help to keep the baby's bottle warm, but they also look a lot prettier than the average plastic bottle. You can make them either in a plain version with a contrasting colored drawstring cord, or a decorated with one with flowers or stars.

If you prefer, you could make a more girly version of the decorations in shades of pink.

Make a few extra stars and flowers with leftover yarn, and use them for decoration in the nursery, or as charming handmade gift tags.

## Sizes

To fit average size baby's bottle

## Yarns

2 x 50g/1¾oz balls of Rowan *Denim* in **MC**
(Memphis 229)

1 x 50g/1¾oz ball of Rowan *Handknit Cotton* in **D**
(Gooseberry 219)

**FOR FLOWERS**

1 x 50g/1¾oz ball of Rowan *4 ply Cotton* in each
of **A** (Bleached 113), **B** (Orchard 120), and **C**
(Cheeky 133)

**FOR STARS**

1 x 50g/1¾oz ball of Rowan *4 ply Cotton* in each
of **A** (Aegean 129), **B** (Opaque 112) and **C**
(Bluebell 136)

## Hooks

Size E-4 (3.5mm) crochet hook
Size G-6 (4mm) crochet hook

## Gauge

**Before washing:** 17 sts and 21 rows to 4in/10cm
measured over sc using MC and size G-6 (4mm)
hook *or size to obtain correct gauge.*

**After washing:** 19 sts and 21 rows to 4in/10cm
measured over sc using MC and size G-6 (4mm)
hook *or size to obtain correct gauge.*

**Note:** Denim will shrink when washed for the first
time. Allowances have been made in the pattern
for shrinkage.

## Abbreviations

See page 117.

## Cover

Using size G-6 (4mm) hook and MC, ch 2.

**Round 1 (RS)** 6 sc in 2nd ch from hook, 1 slip st in first sc, turn. 6 sts.

**Round 2** Ch 1 (does NOT count as st), 2 sc in each sc to end, 1 slip st in first sc, turn. 12 sts.

**Round 3** Ch 1 (does NOT count as st), [1 sc in next sc, 2 sc in next sc] 6 times, 1 slip st in first sc, turn. 18 sts.

**Round 4** Ch 1 (does NOT count as st), [1 sc in each of next 2 sc, 2 sc in next sc] 6 times, 1 slip st in first sc, turn. 24 sts.

**Round 5** Ch 1 (does NOT count as st), [1 sc in each of next 3 sc, 2 sc in next sc] 6 times, 1 slip st in first sc, turn. 30 sts.

**Round 6** Ch 1 (does NOT count as st), [1 sc in each of next 4 sc, 2 sc in next sc] 6 times, 1 slip st in first sc, turn. 36 sts.

**Round 7** Ch 1 (does NOT count as st), 1 sc in each st to end, 1 slip st in first sc, turn.

**Rounds 8 to 44** As round 7.

**Round 45** Ch 1 (does NOT count as st), 1 sc in first sc, [ch 1, skip 1 sc, 1 sc in each of next 2 sc] 11 times, ch 1, skip 1 sc, 1 sc in last sc, 1 slip st in first sc, turn.

**Rounds 46 to 54** As round 7.

Fasten off.

## Finishing

Hot machine wash and tumble dry cover. Do NOT press.

### TIE

Using size G-6 (4mm) hook and D, make a length of chain stitches 15½in/40cm long.

**Row 1** 1 sc in 2nd ch from hook, 1 sc in each ch to end. Fasten off.

Thread tie through holes formed in round 53 and tie ends in a bow.

### OPTIONAL MOTIFS

If required, make either Flower Motifs or Star Motifs as given in the following instructions.

Then sew Flowers or Stars to bottle Cover.

## Flower motifs

### LARGE FLOWER

Using size E-4 (3.5mm) hook and A, ch 6 and join with a slip st to first ch to form a ring.

**Round 1** Ch 1 (does NOT count as st), 16 sc in ring, 1 slip st in first sc. 16 sts.

**Round 2** Ch 1 (does NOT count as st), 1 sc in each of first 2 sc, *[1 sc, ch 9 and 1 sc] in next sc**, 1 sc in each of next 3 sc, rep from * to end, ending last rep at **, 1 sc in last sc, 1 slip st in first sc.

Break off A and join in B.

**Round 3** Ch 1 (does NOT count as st), 1 sc in first sc, *skip 2 sc, [2 hdc, 17 dc and 2 hdc] in next ch loop, skip 2 sc, 1 sc in next sc, rep from * to end, replacing sc at end of last rep with 1 slip st in first sc.

Break off B and join in C.

**Round 4** Ch 1 (does NOT count as st), 1 sc in first sc, *ch 5, skip [2 hdc and 3 dc], 1 sc in next dc, ch 3, 1 slip st in 3rd ch from hook, [ch 5, skip 4 dc, 1 sc in next dc, ch 3, 1 slip st in

*gallery of projects*

3rd ch from hook] twice, ch 5, skip [3 dc and 2 hdc], 1 sc in next sc, rep from * to end, replacing sc at end of last rep with 1 slip st in first sc.

Fasten off.

Make 2 more large flowers—one using B and one using C.

### SMALL FLOWER (make 2)

Using size E-4 (3.5mm) hook and A, ch 6 and join with a slip st to first ch to form a ring.

**Round 1** Ch 1 (does NOT count as st), 16 sc in ring, 1 slip st in first sc. 16 sts.

**Round 2** Ch 1 (does NOT count as st), 1 sc in each of first 2 sc, *[1 sc, ch 5 and 1 sc] in next sc**, 1 sc in each of next 3 sc, rep from * to end, ending last rep at **, 1 sc in last sc, 1 slip st in first sc.

Break off A and join in B.

**Round 3** Ch 1 (does NOT count as st), 1 sc in first sc, *skip 2 sc, [2 hdc, 7 dc and 2 hdc] in next ch loop, skip 2 sc, 1 sc in next sc, rep from * to end, replacing sc at end of last rep with 1 slip st in first sc.

Break off B and join in C.

**Round 4** Ch 1 (does NOT count as st), 1 sc in first sc, *ch 3, skip 2 hdc, 1 sc in next dc, ch 3, 1 slip st in 3rd ch from hook, [ch 3, skip 2 dc, 1 sc in next dc, ch 3, 1 slip st in 3rd ch from hook] twice, ch 3, skip 2 hdc, 1 sc in next sc, rep from * to end, replacing sc at end of last rep with 1 slip st in first sc.

Fasten off.

Embroider French knots around flower center. Sew Flowers randomly onto Cover.

## Star motifs

### LARGE STAR

Using size E-4 (3.5mm) hook and A, ch 10 and join with a slip st to first ch to form a ring.

**Round 1** Ch 4 (counts as first tr), 29 tr in ring, 1 slip st in top of 4 ch at beg of round. 30 sts.

**Round 2** Ch 1 (does NOT count as st), 1 sc in first sc, *ch 6, 1 sc in 2nd ch from hook, 1 hdc in next ch, 1 dc in next ch, 1 tr in next ch, 1 dtr in next ch, skip 4 tr of round 1, 1 sc in next tr, rep from * to end, replacing sc at end of last rep with 1 slip st in first sc.

Fasten off.

Make 2 more large stars—one using B and one using C.

### SMALL STAR (make 2)

Using size E-4 (3.5mm) hook and A, ch 5 and join with a slip st to first ch to form a ring.

**Round 1** Ch 1 (does NOT count as st), 15 sc in ring, 1 slip st in first sc. 15 sts.

**Round 2** Ch 1 (does NOT count as st), 1 sc in first sc, *ch 5, 1 sc in 2nd ch from hook, 1 hdc in next ch, 1 dc in next ch, 1 tr in next ch, skip 2 sc of round 1, 1 sc in next sc, rep from * to end, replacing sc at end of last rep with 1 slip st in first sc.

Fasten off.

Make another small star using B.

Sew Stars randomly onto Cover. Using D, embroider French knots around all Stars.

# gift wrap

• • • • • • • • •

Having finished your handmade crochet project as a present for a new baby, wrap it up in style, lovingly packed in tissue paper in an individual crochet beribboned box, and accompanied by a charming little crochet card with its tiny baby bootees.

These very simple and sweet little projects will give your gift just the right finishing touch and show how much you really care.

Neither of them is difficult to make, so there is no excuse not to make a special effort.

# card

**Size**
Finished shoe is 1¹/₈in/3cm from toe to heel.

**Yarns**
1 x 10g/³/₈oz ball of Coats *Pearl Cotton 8* in either pink 48 or blue 128

**Hook**
Size 6 steel (1.5mm) crochet hook

**Extras**
Blank greeting card
Glue
Tiny amount of toy filling
Organza ribbon

**Gauge**
First 2 rounds measure 1¹/₈in/3cm long and ⁵/₈in/1.5cm at widest point using size 6 steel (1.5mm) hook *or size to obtain correct gauge.*

**Abbreviations**
**sc3tog** = [insert hook in next st, yo and draw loop through] 3 times, yo and draw through all 4 loops on hook.
See also page 117.

**Shoe** (make 2)
Using size 6 steel (1.5mm) hook, ch 8.
**Round 1 (RS)** 2 sc in 2nd ch from hook, 1 sc in each of next 5 ch, 4 sc in last ch, working back along other side of foundation ch: 1 sc in each of next 5 ch, 2 sc in next ch (this is same ch as used for 2 sc at beg of round), 1 slip st in first sc,

turn. 18 sts.

**Round 2** Ch 1 (does NOT count as st), 2 sc in each of first 2 sc, 1 sc in each of next 2 sc, 1 hdc in each of next 2 sc, 2 hdc in next sc, 2 dc in next sc, 3 dc in each of next 2 sc, 2 dc in next sc, 2 hdc in next sc, 1 hdc in each of next 2 sc, 1 sc in each of next 2 sc, 2 sc in each of last 2 sc, 1 slip st in first sc, turn. 30 sts.

**Round 3** Ch 1 (does NOT count as st), working in back loops only of sts of previous round: 1 sc in each st to end, 1 slip st

in first sc, turn.

**Row 4** Ch 1 (does NOT count as st), 1 sc in each of first 16 sc, sc3tog over next 3 sc, turn.

**Row 5** Ch 1 (does NOT count as st), 1 sc in each of first 3 sts, sc3tog over next 3 sc, turn.

**Row 6** Ch 1 (does NOT count as st), 1 sc in each of first 4 sts, 1 sc in each of last 11 sc of round 3, 1 slip st in first sc of row 4, turn.

**Round 7** Ch 1 (does NOT count as st), sc2tog over first 2 sc,

1 sc in each of next 8 sts, sc2tog over next 2 sts, 1 sc in each of next 2 sts, sc2tog over next 2 sts (this is first sc of row 6 and next sc of row 4), 1 sc in each of next 8 sc, sc2tog over last 2 sc, 1 slip st in first sc2tog, turn. 22 sts.

**Round 8** Ch 1 (does NOT count as st), 1 sc in each of first 9 sts, [sc2tog over next 2 sts] twice, 1 sc in each of last 9 sts, 1 slip st in first sc, turn. 20 sts.

**Round 9** Ch 1 (does NOT count as st), 1 sc in each of first 6 sc, ch 3, skip 8 sts, 1 sc in each of last 6 sc, 1 slip st in first sc, turn.

**Round 10** Ch 1 (does NOT count as st), 1 sc in each of first 6 sc, 1 sc in each of next 3 ch, 1 sc in each of last 6 sc, 1 slip st in first sc.

Fasten off.

## Finishing

Do NOT press.

Insert a tiny amount of toy filling in toe of Shoe to support toe area.

Using photograph as a guide, glue Shoes to greeting card. Tie ribbon in a bow and glue to card as shown in photograph.

## lacy ribbon

### Size

Finished ribbon is 1³⁄₈in/3.5cm wide.

### Yarns

1 x 10g/³⁄₈oz ball of Coats *Pearl Cotton 8* in either pink 49 or aqua 167 (This is sufficient for approximately 35½in/90cm of ribbon.)

### Hook

Size 6 steel (1.5mm) crochet hook

### Gauge

One repeat of Ribbon measures 1¼in/3cm using size 6 steel (1.5mm) hook *or size to obtain correct gauge.*

### Abbreviations

See page 117.

### Ribbon

Using size 6 steel (1.5mm) hook, make a ch that is a multiple of 11 ch for each repeat required plus 3 extra ch.

**Row 1 (RS)** 1 sc in 2nd ch from hook, 1 sc in each ch to end, turn.

**Row 2** Ch 1 (does NOT count as st), 1 sc in each of first 2 sc, *ch 3, skip 4 sc, [1 tr, ch 1, 1 tr, ch 1, 1 tr, ch 1, 1 tr, ch 1 and 1 tr] in next sc, ch 3, skip 4 sc, 1 sc in each of next 2 sc, rep from * to end, turn.

**Row 3** Ch 1 (does NOT count as st), 1 sc in first sc, skip 1 sc, *4 sc in next ch sp, [ch 3, 1 sc in next ch sp] 4 times, ch 3, 4 sc in next ch sp**, skip 2 sc, rep from * to end, ending last rep at **, skip 1 sc, 1 sc in last sc, slip st down row-end edge to foundation ch at base of row 1***, ch 1 (does NOT count as st), working in other side of foundation ch, work 1 sc in each ch to end, turn.

**Row 4** As row 2.

**Row 5** As row 3, ending at ***.

Fasten off.

### Finishing

Press lightly on WS following instructions on yarn label. Rosette on boxes in photograph was made up forming 5 loops from crocheted ribbon. (If required, thread fine florist's or jewelry wire through ribbon it to help it hold its shape or stiffen it with starch.)

# practical
# information

· · · · · · · · ·

Crochet is not particularly difficult to master, and the patterns in this book use only relatively simple crochet techniques. However, if you have never crocheted before, you need first to learn how to hold a crochet hook and the yarn correctly and work the basic stitches.

You can crochet with many different kinds of yarn, from special fine crochet cotton through fine wool yarns to string, but amost all the projects in this book use standard knitting yarns.

Crochet starts with a simple foundation chain into which the subsequent stitches are worked. Your ability to crochet depends on the ease with which you can manipulate yarn and hook, and if you have never crocheted before, spend some time practicing the very basic stitches until you achieve a good rhythm and can make evenly formed stitches.

The most common beginner's mistake is to make the stitches too tight. Gauge in crochet (size of stitch) is, as with knitting, crucial to the success of the final piece if it is a fitted item. (See page 116 for more about gauge.)

### Holding the hook and yarn
You can hold the hook in various ways, but one of the simplest and easiest methods is to hold the hook like you would a pencil, as shown below. If you prefer, you can hold the hook in the palm of your hand, between your thumb and first two fingers, like a knife.

To control an even flow of yarn from the ball of working yarn, thread the yarn through the fingers of the left hand (if you are right-handed) with a single twist around the little finger, and with the yarn then running behind the fourth and third fingers, and over the forefinger.

When working crochet, hold the base of the crochet with the first two fingers of the hand holding the yarn. This allows you to create some tension on the yarn, which is essential when pulling the hook and looped yarn through the stitches.

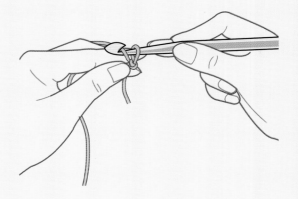

# basic stitches

## First loop

To start to crochet you need to create a first loop on the hook. To do this, form the yarn into a loop, held in place between the thumb and the forefinger, and position the ball end of the yarn behind the loop. Then insert the hook through the center of the loop, catch the yarn strand behind the loop with the crochet hook, and pull it through to create a loop around the hook.

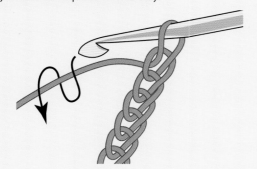

## Foundation chain

To make the foundation chain for your crochet, make your first loop, catch the yarn with the hook, by passing the hook over and under the yarn in a twisting motion as shown by the arrow, then draw the yarn through. Continue to make as many chains as required in this way.

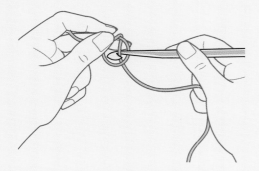

## Slip stitch

The shortest and easiest of the basic crochet stitches is slip stitch. On its own it forms a dense fabric, but it is usually used only as an edging or as a joining stitch.

To work a slip stitch on a foundation chain, insert the hook into the SECOND chain from the hook, catch the yarn with the hook (as shown in making a foundation chain) and draw the yarn through the chain and the loop on the hook to complete the stitch.

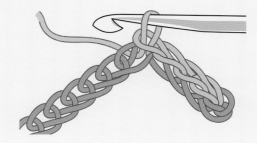

## Fastening off

To fasten off a piece of crochet when it is complete, first cut the thread about 3in (7cm) from the work. Then pass the loose end through the one remaining loop on the hook, and pull tightly. Darn the loose ends into the wrong side of the work, using a blunt-ended yarn needle.

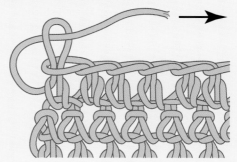

### Single crochet

Single crochet is the most commonly used stitch in crochet and is abbreviated in patterns as sc. It is sometimes known as "plain stitch" and creates a dense, hard-wearing textile.

**HOW TO WORK SINGLE CROCHET**

**1** Make a foundation chain (see page 113), then insert the hook through the SECOND chain from the hook and catch the yarn with the hook (known as yarn over hook or yo).

**2** Draw the hook through the chain so that there are now two loops on the hook.

**3** Wrap the yarn around the hook and draw it through the two loops on the hook—one loop remains on the hook. Work a single crochet in each chain in the same way. On the following rows, work the one turning chain (see below), then work one single crochet in each stitch of the previous row.

#### Working basic stitches in rows

When you turn your crochet work at the end of a row, in order to start the next row you will need to add a specific number of chain stitches—called "turning chains"—to bring the work into the right position to create the stitches for the next row. The chart below gives the number of turning chains required for all the basic crochet stitches.

The turning chains used for half doubles and taller stitches usually count as the first stitch in the row.

**TURNING CHAINS**

| | |
|---|---|
| slip stitch—ch 1 | double crochet—ch 3 |
| single crochet—ch 1 | treble—ch 4 |
| half double—ch 2 | double treble—ch 5 |
| | triple treble—ch 6 |

**1**

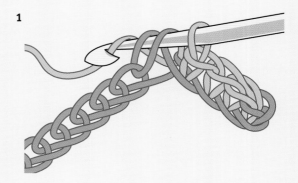

**2**

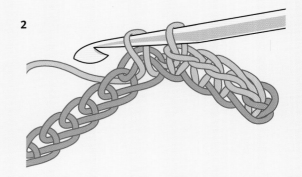

**3**

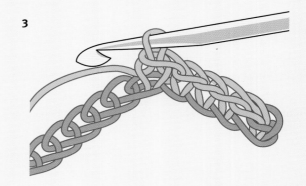

## Half double crochet

Half double is abbreviated as hdc in patterns. It is made in a similar way to single crochet but an additional twist of yarn is made around the hook before the stitch is started. The resulting fabric is slightly more flexible than single crochet.

### HOW TO WORK HALF DOUBLES

**1** Make a foundation chain, then wrap the yarn around the hook and insert the hook through the THIRD chain from the hook.

**2** Wrap the yarn around the hook and draw it through the chain so that there are now three loops on the hook.

**3** Wrap the yarn around the hook again and draw it through all three loops to complete the stitch. Work a half double in each chain. To start the following rows, first work the two turning chains, then skip the first stitch and work one stitch in each of the remaining stitches of the previous row, working the last stitch in the top of the turning chain.

## Double crochet and taller stitches

Double crochet produces a more airy-looking fabric that is softer than either single or half double crochet.

To work a double crochet, yo and insert the hook through the FOURTH chain from the hook. Yo and draw the yarn through the chain. Yo and draw the yarn through the first two loops on the hook. Yo and draw the yarn through the two remaining loops on the hook. One loop remains on the hook. Work a double crochet in each chain in the same way. Work the following rows as for half doubles, but make three turning chains.

The taller basic stitches—trebles, double trebles, and triple trebles—are worked like doubles, but start with two, three, or four wraps around the hook instead of only one.

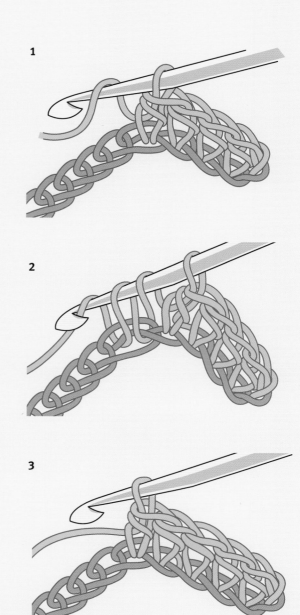

**1**

**2**

**3**

*basic stitches*

## Working in rounds

If you want to create a piece of crochet fabric that is circular, such as the base of the pots on pages 52–57, you will have to start with a chain circle. This is created quite simply from a suitable length of foundation chains that are then linked end to end to form a ring.

Make a foundation chain (see page 113) of the specified number of chains. Insert the hook into the first chain worked, catch the yarn with hook (**1**) and draw it through the loop on the hook to form a ring (**2**). Then crochet in rounds as instructed.

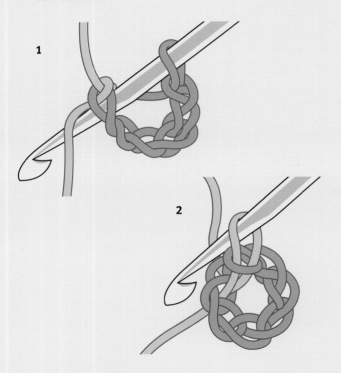

## A professional finish

There are a number of useful tips and techniques that will help you create a professionally finished crocheted garment or accessory.

### GAUGE

The first is to ensure that your crochet is to the correct size. You do this by measuring gauge, which enables you to check that your crochet will be to the correct size. In the pattern instructions, you will be told how many rows and stitches are required to achieve an identical size to that given in the pattern.

To check that your crochet stitches are a similar size, crochet a square approximately 5in (13cm) in size. Count the number of rows and stitches across 4in (10cm) in this square. If these are identical to those given in the pattern, that is fine. If you have more rows and stitches, use a larger size hook; if you have fewer rows and stitches, use a smaller size hook.

### BLOCKING

When you have finished the various parts of the crocheted item, they need to be pressed. Check the yarn label for any pressing instructions.

Then pin out each piece of crocheted fabric (wrong side up) to the correct measurements—this is called "blocking." Place a clean, damp cloth over the crochet and lightly press with an iron. Avoid pressing raised textures as they will be flattened. Remove the pins when the crochet is completely dry.

### SEAMS

To join two pieces of a crochet together, you will need to stitch them using a blunt-ended yarn needle and a strand of yarn from the garment. If the yarn is thick, untwist and use a single thread.

Backstitch seams work well with crochet, but overcasting stitches can be used as well.

To work a backstitch seam, place the two pieces of crochet right sides together and pin in position. Sew together with a row of backstitches, worked one stitch in from the edge.

# working from patterns

## Crochet abbreviations

The following are the abbreviations used in the patterns in this book. Special abbreviations are given with individual patterns.

| | |
|---|---|
| **alt** | alternate |
| **beg** | begin(ning) |
| **CC** | contrasting color |
| **ch** | chain(s) |
| **ch sp** | chain space |
| **cm** | centimeter(s) |
| **cont** | continu(e)(ing) |
| **dc** | double crochet |
| **dec** | decreas(e)(ing) |
| **DK** | double knitting (a medium-weight yarn) |
| **dtr** | double treble |
| **foll** | follow(s)(ing) |
| **g** | gram(s) |
| **hdc** | half double |
| **in** | inch(es) |
| **inc** | increas(e)(ing) |
| **m** | meter(s) |
| **MC** | main color |
| **mm** | millimeter(s) |
| **oz** | ounce(s) |
| **patt** | pattern; *or* work in pattern |
| **rem** | remain(s)(ing) |
| **rep** | repeat(s)(ing) |
| **RS** | right side |
| **sc** | single crochet |
| **sc2tog** | [insert hook into next st, yo and draw loop through] twice, yo and draw through all 3 loops on hook (one stitch decreased) |
| **sp** | space |
| **slip st** | slip stitch |
| **st(s)** | stitch(es) |
| **tog** | together |
| **tr** | treble crochet |
| **WS** | wrong side |
| **yd** | yard(s) |
| **yo** | yarn over (hook) |

* Repeat instructions after asterisk or between asterisks as many times as instructed.

[ ] Repeat instructions inside square brackets as many times as instructed; or work all instructions inside square brackets into same place.

## Crochet terminology

Crochet terminology is different in the US and UK. This book is written with US terminology. Here are the UK equivalents:

| US | UK |
|---|---|
| single crochet (sc) | double crochet (dc) |
| half double crochet (hdc) | half treble crochet (htr) |
| double crochet (dc) | treble crochet (tr) |
| treble (tr) | double treble (dtr) |
| double treble (dtr) | triple treble (ttr *or* trtr) |
| triple treble (trtr) | quadruple treble (qtr) |
| yarn over hook (yo) | yarn round hook (yrh) |
| skip | miss |
| slip stitch (sl st) | slip stitch (ss) |

## Sizes in patterns

In patterns that have a choice of sizes, the smallest size comes first and the remaining sizes follow inside parentheses ( ). Where there is only one set of figures, it applies to all sizes. Be sure to follow the same size throughout the pattern.

# yarns

The following list covers the yarns used in this book. All the information was correct at the time of publication, but yarn companies change their products frequently and cannot absolutely guarantee that the yarn types or shades used will be available when you come to use these patterns.

For the best results, always use the yarn specified in your pattern. Contact the distributors on page 120 to find a supplier of Rowan yarn near you. For countries not listed, contact the main office in the UK.

The yarn label information given below provides the recommended gauge for knitting. You can use this information to find a yarn of an equivalent thickness when looking for a substitute yarn. To calculate quantities of substitute yarns, always decide on the number of balls you need by ball length (yardage) rather than by ball weight.

Always check the yarn label for care instructions.

### COATS PEARL COTTON 8
This is a lightweight twisted embroidery thread, available in shops selling embroidery threads.

### ROWAN CALMER
A medium-weight cotton-mix yarn; 75 percent cotton, 25 percent acrylic/microfiber; approximately 175yd/160m per 50g/1¾oz ball; recommended gauge—21 sts and 30 rows to 4in/10cm measured over stockinette stitch using size 8 (5mm) knitting needles.

### ROWAN COTTON GLACE
A lightweight cotton yarn; 100 percent cotton; approximately 126yd/115m per 50g/1¾oz ball; recommended gauge—23 sts and 32 rows to 4in/10cm measured over stockinette stitch using size 3–5 (3.25–3.75mm) knitting needles.

### ROWAN DENIM
A medium-weight cotton yarn; 100 percent cotton; approximately 102yd/93m per 50g/1¾oz ball; recommended gauge—20 sts and 28 rows (before washing) and 20 sts and 32 rows (after washing) to 4in/10cm measured over stockinette stitch using size 6 (4mm) knitting needles.

### ROWAN 4 PLY COTTON
A lightweight cotton yarn; 100 percent cotton; approximately 186yd/170m per 50g/1¾oz ball; recommended gauge—27–29 sts and 37–39 rows to 4in/10cm measured over stockinette stitch using size 2–3 (3–3.25mm) knitting needles.

### ROWAN HANDKNIT COTTON
A medium-weight 100 percent cotton yarn; approximately 93yd/85m per 50g/1¾oz ball; recommended gauge—19–20 sts and 28 rows to 4in/10cm measured over stockinette stitch using size 6–7 (4–4.5mm) knitting needles.

### ROWAN RYC CASHCOTTON 4 PLY
A lightweight cotton-mix yarn; 35 percent cotton, 25 percent polyamide, 18 percent angora, 13 percent viscose, 9 percent cashmere; approximately 197yd/180m per 50g/1¾oz ball; recommended gauge—28 sts and 36 rows to 4in/10cm measured over stockinette stitch using size 3 (3.25mm) knitting needles.

### ROWAN RYC CASHSOFT BABY DK
A medium-weight wool-and-cashmere-mix yarn; 57 percent extra fine merino wool, 33 percent microfiber, 10 percent

cashmere; approximately 142yd/130m per 50g/1¾oz ball; recommended gauge—22 sts and 30 rows to 4in/10cm measured over stockinette stitch using size 6 (4mm) knitting needles.

### ROWAN RYC CASHSOFT BABY 4 PLY

A lightweight wool-and-cashmere-mix yarn; 57 percent extra fine merino wool, 33 percent microfiber, 10 percent cashmere; approximately 197yd/180m per 50g/1¾oz ball; recommended gauge—28 sts and 36 rows to 4in/10cm measured over stockinette stitch using size 3 (3.25mm) knitting needles.

### ROWAN RYC CASHSOFT DK

A medium-weight wool-and-cashmere-mix yarn; 57 percent extra fine merino wool, 33 percent microfiber, 10 percent cashmere; approximately 142yd/130m per 50g/1¾oz ball; recommended gauge—22 sts and 30 rows to 4in/10cm measured over stockinette stitch using size 6 (4mm) knitting needles.

### ROWAN RYC CASHSOFT 4 PLY

A lightweight wool-and-cashmere-mix yarn; 57 percent extra fine merino wool, 33 percent microfiber, 10 percent cashmere; approximately 197yd/180m per 50g/1¾oz ball; recommended gauge—28 sts and 36 rows to 4in/10cm measured over stockinette stitch using size 3 (3.25mm) knitting needles.

## author's acknowledgments

I would like to thank the little children who modeled for this book, Amelia, Mia, and Ellie, their mums, and also my own daughter, Maddie. They were all stars! I would also like to thank Susan, John, and Anne for getting it all together on the page, Sue for her crochet and pattern writing, Sally for her editing, and the team at Rowan for their support. I would also like to thank Julian and our children for their patience while we invaded the house with small children and projects!

# yarn suppliers

Below is the list of overseas distributors for Rowan handknitting yarns; contact them for suppliers near you/in your country or contact the main office in the UK or the Rowan website for any others.

See pages 118 and 119 for yarn information.

USA
Westminster Fibers Inc.,
4 Townsend West, Suite 8, Nashua, NH 03063.
Tel: +1 (603) 886-5041/5043.
E-mail: rowan@westminsterfibers.com

AUSTRALIA
Australian Country Spinners, 314 Albert Street,
Brunswick, Victoria 3056.
Tel: (03) 9380 3888.
E-mail: sales@auspinners.com.au

BELGIUM
Pavan, Meerlaanstraat 73, B9860 Balegem
(Oosterzele).
Tel: (32) 9 221 8594.
E-mail: pavan@pandora.be

CANADA
Diamond Yarn, 9697 St Laurent, Montreal,
Quebec H3L 2N1.
Tel: (514) 388 6188.
Diamond Yarn (Toronto), 155 Martin Ross, Unit 3,
Toronto, Ontario M3J 2L9.
Tel: (416) 736-6111.
E-mail: diamond@diamondyarn.com

FINLAND
Coats Opti Oy, Ketjutie 3, 04220 Kerava.
Tel: (358) 9 274 871.
Fax: (358) 9 2748 7330.
E-mail: coatsopti.sales@coats.com

FRANCE
Elle Tricot, 8 Rue du Coq, 67000 Strasbourg.
Tel: (33) 3 88 23 03 13.
E-mail: elletricot@agat.net
www.elletricote.com

GERMANY
Wolle & Design, Wolfshovener Strasse 76,
52428 Julich-Stetternich.
Tel: (49) 2461 54735.
E-mail: Info@wolleunddesign.de
www.wolleunddesign.de
Coats GMbH, Eduardstrasse 44, D-73084 Salach.
Tel: (49) 7162/14-346.  www.coatsgmbh.de

HOLLAND
de Afstap, Oude Leliestraat 12, 1015 AW
Amsterdam.
Tel: (31) 20 6231445.

HONG KONG
East Unity Co Ltd, Unit B2,
7/F Block B, Kailey Industrial Centre,
12 Fung Yip Street, Chai Wan.
Tel: (852) 2869 7110.

ICELAND
Storkurinn, Laugavegi 59, 101 Reykjavik.
Tel: (354) 551 8258.
E-mail: malin@mmedia.is

ITALY
D.L. srl, Via Piave 24–26, 20016 Pero, Milan.
Tel: (39) 02 339 10 180.

JAPAN
Puppy Co. Ltd., T151-0051, 3-16-5 Sendagaya,
Shibuyaku, Tokyo.
Tel: (81) 3 3490 2827.
E-mail: info@rowan-jaeger.com

KOREA
Coats Korea Co. Ltd., 5F Kuckdong B/D, 935-40
Bangbae-Dong, Seocho-Gu, Seoul.
Tel: (82) 2 521 6262.
Fax: (82) 2 521 5181.

NORWAY
Coats Knappehuset A/S, Postboks 63, 2801
Gjovik.
Tel: (47) 61 18 34 00.

SINGAPORE
Golden Dragon Store, 101 Upper Cross Street
#02-51, People's Park Centre, Singapore.
Tel: (65) 6 5358454.

SOUTH AFRICA
Arthur Bales PTY, P.O. Box 44644, Linden 2104.
Tel: (27) 11 888 2401.

SPAIN
Oyambre, Pau Claris 145, 80009 Barcelona.
Tel: (34) 670 011957.
E-mail: comercial@oyambreonline.com

SWEDEN
Wincent, Norrtullsgatan 65, 113 45 Stockholm.
Tel: (46) 8 33 70 60.
E-mail: wincent@chello.se

TAIWAN
Laiter Wool Knitting Co. Ltd., 10-1 313 Lane, Sec
3, Chung Ching North Road, Taipei.
Tel: (886) 2 2596 0269.
Mon Cher Corporation, 9F No 117 Chung Sun First
Road, Kaoshiung. Tel: (886) 7 9711988.

UK
Rowan Yarns, Green Lane Mill,
Holmfirth, West Yorkshire HD9 2DX.
Tel: 01484 681881.
E-mail: mail@knitrowan.com
www.knitrowan.com